MW01591406

Connecticut River Review

Copyright © 2023 by the Connecticut Poetry Society

Connecticut River Review
2023

Connecticut River Review is a national poetry journal sponsored by the Connecticut Poetry Society. All rights revert to the authors on publication.

Editors: Ginny Lowe Connors, Debbie Gilbert, and John Surowiecki
Additional Readers: Garrett Phelan and Debora Kuan
Book & Cover Design: Cindy Stewart
Cover Photo: Dave Boardman, pixabay.com

ISBN: 979-8-9855442-8-2

Copyright © 2023 by the **Connecticut Poetry Society**
www.ctpoetry.net

Contents

Dennis Barone

In New England

An old tree leans as two old
horses groan and smoke rises
then disappears. This season
has not been blest. This

year too much rain and for
far too long. No snow. Still
Jedidiah checks his taps and
tries his best. He accepts

what he can get and then
takes it to boil and eventual
sweetness. I'm inside trying
Jed's craft on the cakes that

I have made and, yes, syrup
is so much sweeter than life.

Maria Berardi

Multiverse

It is all the shadow-lives that disturb,
being again in that place

after all this time,
after hard-won whatever

wisdom is, after desirelessness itself.
After practicing for death

every day, in that spiritual way,
very quiet, only breathing,

after all this training—
still the shadow-lives disturb:

the life where the other one lived,
the life where there were both.

The life that was a room
where the woman started weeping and has never stopped.

The life where they lived in their ideal place.
The life where they were not so fearful of the future.

The life, though, where the drinking never stopped.
That one, too. The weeping that seeped through

until it was a sea, a no-boundary of brokenness,
broken psyches, broken trust. That life, too.

And then the life without chronic illness,
imagine, where care was not so relentless,

where everybody
slept through the night.

All these ghost lives passing right through
the warm body; the chill of them,

the stopped-ness. Specimens in jars.
Or roaming out there—

met out there—
disturbing this life,

this only life, dissolving
as they become old weather.

Tiffany Bergin

Ariadne Answers Us from Naxos

So I gave up my country.
It was a leaky vessel anyway,
always knocking about its neighbors.
Give me a coracle any day:
a map, an oar, and some
disobedient destination.
For what's a country if it's not
fit enough to lie in? Give me
this craggy outcrop where I was thrown.
I no longer require blossom.
Yes, he left me anyway, but
I did not give up my country for him.
Mythologize him, but leave me be.
Myths are leaky vessels to lie in.

paul Bluestein

Out of the Frame

In 1885, Winslow Homer painted me into "The Fog Warning"
and left me to struggle on my own.
For more than a hundred years,
I've hung in a Boston museum, rowing this flimsy dory
through his ominous gray-green ocean and I'm tired of it.
My cold hands are blistered
and the halibut in the stern began to rot long ago.
The patrons who come to see Homer's painting
imagine I am looking out at the fog or the mother ship
floating on the horizon, They have no idea
I'm looking at the gallery wall across this stormy sea,
thinking it's long past time to get out of this painting
and off this stinking boat.
On the opposite wall is a beckoning Gaugin—
three women at play on a tropical; beach,
one of them perched naked on a horse.
I could row my boat over to that beach,
climb out and say hello.
After decades with only one another's company,
they might welcome a guest.
Old Winslow's been dead many years,
so he won't object to me slipping away
and I doubt many museum visitors would notice I've gone.
Instead of living the solitary life of a fisherman,
I could dig my fingers into warm sand,
eat papayas ripe from the tree and maybe fall in love.
Yes, it's time to leave New England for a more gentle shore.
I just wish that instead of these damn halibut,
Winslow had painted me an apple for the horse.

John J. Brugaletta

To My Unborn Child

Presumptuous of me, my words to you,
as much so as the home talk of the traveler
worlds away. We do not share assumptions.
Your air is aqueous, your eyes firm,
gravity a promise that makes no sense.
You move in your Ptolemaic sphere
in that purest of directions, the spiral,
making of it encapsulated space.

Intergalactic alien, you are us, your mother,
me and my former selves:
the stonemason and the grafter of trees,
thief and priest,
dog-man with cocked leg and honest statesman.

Beyond all that, you come from past
all nomads, savages, animals, amoebas.
You come from chance, which may be God:
the fortunate encounter and the spark.

In you I have returned to nothing.
In you we all have tossed into the air
this house of sticks, ourselves,
and watched, like diviners of kings,
the pieces falling into patterns
original and eternal.

Nothingness has been mute,
and will be so till you arrive.

Anne Champion

Happy Birthday, Dear Rapist

Sometimes I imagine the day you were born. I was 7,
somewhere in Kalamazoo, Michigan, watching my father

paint model planes. *Tell me about girls who flew, Dad.*

If you try to be a girl who flies, no man will love you.

Somewhere in Mathis, Texas, you took
your first gulp of air and choked, unleashing

your first cry of many cries, as your mother's palm cupped
your backside, the first time of many times.

Nobody knew I'd be a writer. Nobody knew
you'd be a stalker, a rapist who drugs women.

No way anyone could've known: that infant's wail
would be the demonic possession of every pronoun I write.

That pursed pout would be the sleep paralysis apparition,
its teeth to my tits every morning, hissing, *You'll never fly.*

Robert Cording

Snowy Egret in the Rain

I am inside sitting by a bank of windows,
Watching a small pond where a snowy egret,

For over an hour, has been standing in a heavy rain,
As unreacting as the stones that rim the water.

It can't fish, the water a craze of zigzagging lines
Darting like fish. At first I imagined the egret

Choosing this form of suffering, but the egret is
Buddha-still, peaceful, as if it were being drenched

By some life-giving essence. If I knew how to read egret,
I'd say it almost seems to welcome this break

From paying attention. It certainly doesn't ask,
What should I be doing? It waits.

Time is meaningless. It is raining. The rain will stop.
The water will become a single plane of light.

The sun will light the water all the way to the bottom.
The tall Royal palms at the pond's other end will lay down

Their perfect reflections as if extending themselves
To the bird outside my window. The snowy egret will fish.

Mark Cox

Music Box

For Ralph Angel

Everything's just peachy, comes the world report: all clear. We are not pirouetting on the tip of time's scalpel; we are not screwing deeper into the ground's veneer. It is just the fleeting dance we do until the delicate box closes, having learned now to bow before hurting ourselves.

Today is Thursday once again and the man next door is off to get his mail. He will wander back reading, as is his wont to do, his wizened leashed dachshund dog sniffing at the leaves. The breeze passes over our shrubs and still they stand. A wary sparrow peers from them but we shouldn't call it hiding.

Yes, we have learned how to brace for the brief plunge toward otherness. We have learned to keep our eyes open to the dark, even if it doesn't matter. We see best what cannot be seen, and this is always the case.

In the caves of our past, flames flickered on the rough walls. Fear grew there beyond reason and all sense of proportion. Our shadows have always been bigger than we are, the house lights shining up as they do, not down.

It would make sense to be offered a tune now. Something simple and genuine, a tale of longing fulfilled. Something to do with a childhood nightlight, a mother's cool palm. Whatever it is, it will have to be a memory wound long ago.

Such a blessing might be broadcast from just about anywhere. We receive it on this bureau with no clue wherefrom it issues, which ancient satellite or lofty transmission tower. On and off like a warning beacon, the message beams. Once all is said, one has no choice but to choose. Call it grace, call it wonder, just, as they say, keep it calling.

Dallas Crow

Another Mystery Train

This one is 16 engines long.
That's it. No hoppers, coal cars,
box cars, flat cars, cattle cars,
container cars, tankers, no club car.
Nothing but 16 yellow engines
blazoned with American flags
in far western Wyoming (almost
Idaho), 8 facing north, 8 facing
south. No rock n roll out here.
No Jerry Lee to liberate us
or Elvis to save us. Just
a whole lotta sage going on.
It's the summer of '22,
the end of the empire visible
on the horizon if you're looking
for it. Otherwise, whole lotta
sage going on. I've been driving
down this road 50, 60, 70 years.
Nearly everything alive when
I started is gone now. There's
still plastic, a little neon here
and there, and a train in western
Wyoming that's 16 engines long.

Dallas Crow

For Jo

There's a divot in my heart.
Bob's left Jo,
and I don't know what to do
with my hands

or heart or soul.
You count on certain things;
you think they're gold.

To be flayed
and then to be forced
to walk out in the world

among the living
day after day after
day—it's torture.

There is no poultice
for a wound that large.
Time heals, they assure you.

It also abrades,
grates, rends.

You are torn, my friend,
frayed, sucker punched
by life, gutted by love.

Let sunflowers, let lakes,
let islands, let a blossoming son,
let rain, let friends…

I, who don't pray,
pray *Let love*…

John Cullen

The Fall

In the 60's kids stewed comics all night
by flashlight, long after bedtime demands
by parents pounding stairs and shaking
the world like intergalactic robots.
Green Lantern pledged universal allegiance.
Spider Man, dodging webbing from cigars
and a crew cut, untangled innocence,
then despaired at silk's weight.
Superman raced frame by frame, but cloaked
an alien essence and childhood stories.
Huddled under tents, faces blanketed
in idealism recognized themselves.
Playboy and the Beach Boys couldn't interfere
with recruitment to the Justice League,
and Vietnam's slog into muddy debt
failed to drown their belief in the power.
Each page turned certain as the sun's rotation,
but in the end revealed a lonely unfolding
of the planet's gaseous pinprick, the solar system
inside each molecule.

Patrick Daly

Arms

What is the hope for suffering if Guan Yin's thousand arms are not
   enough?
Suffering is uncountable—
the suffering of each is only this, and like no other
the one tree in a field.

What can we do with this one tree of suffering?
A fool might try to uproot it, or one who loves
all trees might water it.
But when the time comes when one has to climb into it,
when one comes alone to the lone tree of *Never was grief like mine*,
how strange to find many are already gathering and settling into it,
   like crows at dusk,
to drink in the darkness as it comes on, the blackness—

I can't see
but I will try to imagine something good at finding its way in the
   dark—
mycelia twined in the roots, fungus so good at finding its way
to feed on and feed the tree you might think it was love if you felt it.
They say faith needs not knowing. Nothingness also does,
so I may be a fool to say love is a growth of darkness,
a creature of arms, thousands of arms,
enough arms.

*The name Guan Yin (also spelled Kuan Yin) is a short form of Kuan-shi Yin,
meaning roughly "Hearing the Cries of the World." A Buddhist legend says that
when Guan Yin tried to reach out to all those whose cries she could hear, her two
arms shattered and the Buddha replaced them with a thousand arms. I learned about
the remarkable properties of mycelia from Merlin Sheldrake's book* Entangled Life. *
The quotation in italics is from George Herbert's poem "The Sacrifice."*

Patrick Daly

Fog Stanzas

1.
Nothing needs to be decided
just yet.

2. *Fog and sequoia:*
"Let me show you heaven,"
he says, pointing.
"Let me help you forget,"
she replies, silk falling
on silk, "why you ever wanted to go there."

3.
Remember that moment—
just before the river touched your body
and cold took you in one gulp, like an oyster—

a gate opening
between one life and the next:

there are no gates in the fog.
It hangs above the street
like someone lying awake
changing and changing his mind.

4. *A question for the fog:*
The pianist, rapt,
playing to her unborn child,
the child swimming close to listen—
how could Bach sound
without the notion of light?

5.
We are all still one
breathing creature.

6. *The poet:*
Four weeks lost in rain—
but come the fog,
she puts out buckets.
Soon she pulls on a wisp
and begins to knit, plying fast
before the sun finds her.

7. *What the fog needs:*
Feet.
The luxury of strong legs
and a direction to go in.

8. *Darwin, Freud, Einstein…*
They said
This is how the world is,
This is how the world is, we replied
but even if it is only
how the mind is, and the mind, we know, is only
fog shining in light—
still it is good to know
how the mind is.

9.
Poor Hamlet, all he wanted—
my father the fog was everywhere—
all I wanted
was a moment to think.

Jim Daniels

Sand Bar, Lake Huron

Every rock eventually succumbs to erosion and will become sand with time.

On the beach, hefty rocks clacked
against each other near shore
in their ancient dedicated work
of becoming sand. For years
we were only allowed to wade
in ankle-deep under the fearful
gaze of our grandfather
who could not swim.

We stood wobbly on those uneven
stones, watching others swim out
to the sand bar and miraculously
stand up in the shallows,
a mirage of possibility
even after we had passed our lessons
in the school pool back home.

Until we passed our lessons
to drive cars, and he could no longer
and we parked him in a beach chair
anchored with stones
and swam out to the sand bar ourselves
standing up in the cold freeze of wind
to wave to him on shore

from our island. Separated by the lake's
cool clear water, all he could do
was wave back from his own drowning
while somewhere in between us, beneath us,
the water was doing its work
stone turning to sand
at some shifting point
in the depths we swam over.

Jim Davis

Ten Years After the Hysterectomy

My unborn brother has a ghost
man on second. I throw crabapples from the sewer
cap, he swings a picket of the neighbor's fence.
He has a scar on his heart for the dead dog too,
a blue pellet gun in a pillowcase in the closet
behind his church shoes. He sticks out his tongue
when he juggles & he can feel when July's moon
haloes in his firework eyes, my mother's hazel.
We hassle my father. We play *Prisoner of War*
& *Peter Pan* &   run in cursive
to collect   lightning
bugs for a jar   to disturb
the night beside   two bunked beds.
If the ghost man ever made it home, our mother
would read us *Romulus & Gretel*, before laying
her head down behind the wall covered in blue
Champion pennants & Frank Thomas posters,
howl gently. She would hear us laughing & if we
were fast asleep my mother would come in, crack
a window, set two water glasses on the desk for me
& the shadow rounding third with a bar of soap.

Emma DeNaples

Poem for My Mother

I won't tell you how long I stayed up that night you broke the kitchen window/ lying underneath the table with my alice doll/ waiting for you to come home as wintertime air filled the room like a hush./ I won't tell you why I really wanted that electric toothbrush when I was thirteen/ although maybe you already know/ and I won't tell you about the white fox/bluegill/black mold. the cat scratched the sofa cushion once and it opened like a wound/ I turned it over before you could see./ I knew you resented us for being just like those sludgey kids/ the ones you looked down on back in vermont/ but I'd never tell you that/ either. I'd never tell you about all the times nyla laid me down in the marsh/ in the meadow/ not about how she used to breathe into my neck while we slept/ or how she spread me open./ I won't tell you about the raspberry jam/cookie cutter/empty kettle/ and I won't tell you how emptied I feel when I remember that you sang to me every night for ten years/ every night that you were there, anyway./ I won't tell you about the sandstone/ about what we buried/ you blamed clutter when things went missing/ you'd have never even thought to ask./ I can't tell you what I let him to do me./ all the times I woke up to it./ and how I never said a word./ you weren't the kind of mother to warn me about those things/ but I like to think you would have been angry/sad/sorry anyway./ I didn't tell you when that woman cut off my hair/ and you didn't notice. I won't tell you about the carnival off the side of the highway/ and I won't tell you about the tea/blood/ mucus stain on my white sheets,/ and I won't ask you what it was about my eleventh birthday that made your song stop./ I won't admit to you/ that I still bite my fingernails. I won't tell you/ that I'm still under that table.

Jeanine DeRusha

Today I Will Write a Joyful Poem

I will note the bright green inchworm
drifting down a thread onto the bench beside me

and admire up-close the complicated bloom
of the pink bleeding heart,

the bow-legged amble of my dog on his lead,
the birds – a robin, a mourning dove – bathing

in dirty water ponding on the pool cover.
Not because I'm unaware that children

were shot to death at an elementary school
yesterday and that all they'll miss is flushed

into the black hole their absence will leave.
Not because I'm unaware that everything is living

around some dark mass in our galaxy,
which I don't understand, not even a little,

or why we have to exist this close to the end
of it all. I just need to write a joyful poem today,

far from the cusp of falling down
any uncovered well. Just for a moment

I'll gaze on the white, straight teeth of my son
whose braces were removed this morning.

Those bright, clean pearls. My God, how the blue sky
casts over us, a cerulean umbrella,

protecting us from nothing. I'll only admire the hue,
not its merciless beauty which delivers, indifferently,

and without regard to loss,
a spring day.

Andrea Janelle Dickens

koi pond in melt

they rise like questions
                             & sink again down deep.
their clocks are confused; it's not their time quite yet.
midwinter spring:

                         the third day koi ascend
unsure if they should stay below or seek for food
among the thaw.

                         translucent edge-ice
still limes the paving stones.
                                 its thin sheet cracks,
becomes gray floes.
                         the fish below break top,
nudge green-blue ice with warm-orange, groping mouths,
stir winter-dark waters, where flat shadow reaches
to secret depths that winter cannot reach.

they don't need to surface, except:
                                 the sun.
their false spring blinds them
                         as they quit their cave.

so they loiter, ineffective, just bobbing:
until the snows return and send them back.

Chase Dimock

Echolocation for Elderly Dogs

My dog can no longer detect
the direction of my voice.
She peeks her head sideways
inquiring through my door frame,
eyes glassy like ancient marbles
excavated from the desert
that have seen time immemorial
but now see nothing.

When I call her in, my voice
echoes in dimensions only
perceptible in dementia
and I am carried out of my body
into another room. Her ears
now have the acoustics of an old church
where the ceiling slants to misdirect hymns
back down to the congregation, mimicking
the thundering voice of God above.

As though I am a ventriloquist
throwing my voice down the hall,
she runs opposite my room to find me,
just a dummy made of shadow
propped in the corner.
Like a submarine's sonar
confused by a lonely whale
for a potential mate,
she scratches at the floor,
believing I had been buried
under a lawn of worn berber.

But when I think of how I've paced
down the hall, sweat, pheromones,
and dead skin seeded into the carpet,
I am as much there for her as anywhere.
The residue of anxiety populates me

everywhere, a house of mirrors
built for a snout that bloops blindly,
but trustingly into the walls.

When she digs down to the hardwood below
her paws will pound like knuckles knocking
on a casket. Every dog is an archeologist
and I hope my skeleton will offer
the shinbone that I cannot.

Dante Di Stefano

Imperative Self-Portrait as My Great-Grandfather

Carry a *Commedia*
      you can't read as you recross
Atlantics and ascend steel
          skeletons of skyscrapers
      unbuilt in the morning light
of the early twentieth
      century, continually
rising across Manhattan,
          shadows falling on diners
      and factories upstate. Hold
a family history
      in the stressed syllables of
often mispronounced surnames.

          Lose the hundred dialects
      and vernaculars of home.

Embrace the illusory
      promise rolling so swiftly
from every preamble
          in this new land. Forget what
      made the old country holy.

Invite the pilgrimages
      of your descendants to take
root in the loam of your red
          blood cells, adjudicating
      the cerulean the stars
are stitched against on the flag.

      Deny the myths that will spring
from your toil and tears and sweat.

          Remember you are your own
      ancestor and progeny,
praetor of sunlight, mailman

carrying dead letters to
relatives who no longer know
           the same cursive tongue you speak
    in the wrecked coliseums
of a long-fallen empire
     you hold still in your heartbeat.

Sara Ries Dziekonski

What the Birds Know

One day, when you sit, and your feet touch
the floor, pressing it with your history of steps,
I'll show you the photograph of you

from the night we kept you out way too late.
You're in the ruana that daddy brought home
from the market, holding your yellow truck—*truckery*,

you call it, and who am I to correct you
when my gringa tongue stumbles on rolling r's,
and I repeat and repeat but *still* can't say certain words.

For a thick dictionary of time, we just stood on that damp
dirt road and watched the pigeons roost in the eaves of Iglesia
del Carmen, the church built in 1850, and the silence shuffled

their feathers, our faces glowing in the sconces' yellow lights,
bodies bundled in bird language, so that we did not move,
nor speak, just raised our chins to see

la evidencia of magic, or mystery, the thing
that no one really has the words for:
what the birds know.

Kathleen Ellis

Night Flying

When the waiting room at Logan Airport emptied
after midnight, I curled up on a bench,

on a hard wooden bench,
on a bench that smelled like travelers,

with one eye open, keeping watch on the clean-up crew
erasing the presence of bodies arriving and departing.

I slept until a woman who only spoke Spanish
and carried a pail of soapy water, shook me awake

by the shoulder of my winter coat, and asked
me to move, *Por favor, ahorita!* What I thought

she said was *You've arrived at your destination.*
Around me, the faces of another country

were crossing borders, offering passports and green cards
as evidence of their existence. And I sat up on the bench,

stretching my body into the upright position. I pulled
on my boots with my documents stashed in their sides

for safekeeping. And only a woman holding her mop
in one hand and wiping the other on her gingham apron

to give me a hand, knew I'd come such a long way
to translate one flight into another.

David Epstein

A Cosmic Bus Stop

In the dust at the edges of the universe,
where being's baseboards gather shadow,

and where I go when you are far away,
—this night, with its diffuse array of hedgerow

that is only the stuttery gait of light slowing down,
—there, among heliotrope and hyacinth,

where the orphan stars carom like billiard balls
off a gravity so slackened that an idea needs traction.

I will wait for you. It isn't warm so close to zed.
Time itself is waiting too: that's how late you are,

your usual, because the worn down worlds have always waited
for beauty, turning acid oceans into mists

reaching from their horizons to the canopy
above what light is here: stand with me, by me,

touching hips. Yes we get to walk away, out of this,
out of cradle-shoes, out of mystic gin, past lives

cawing like baby gulls, to the nether
where you never have to call me,

only lift your wrist to find the back of my hand.
Because the light has slowed so,

and the interstellar breezes are lapping at the void;
because the fifth force in the universe emerges here

(weaker than newborn kittens, often mistaken for laughter)
you turn to me and say, with gesture,

Go. Go and get me a sieve for evening,
I want to keep the last light from leaving.

James Finnegan

Always Looking Down

He was always looking down,
he navigated the pavement by constellations
of broken windshield glass.
He knew where the rabbit slumped
into the culvert.

He was always looking down,
along shoulders of crushed gravel,
following serpentine lines of poured tar.
I have seen him staring intently
at marsh marigolds in the ditch.

A horn-blast from a passing truck,
the blackbird's rusty-hinge note,
nothing could get him to raise his head.
I think he was looking for the shadow
of the person he once was,
or a sudden opening in the earth.

James Finnegan

Not Fallen, Only Tilting

To live in a shitty beach town
where the cars go by too fast
on the highway that abuts
the beach parking lot, but a wind
comes off the ocean in the evening,
and it's walking distance
to the wooden pier,
which is about a quarter-mile long,
in need of repair, 'only tilting'
as the town councilor said
before voting down
a tax levy to prop it level,
and if you make it out to the end
after having been drinking,
always some men will be fishing
until dark, not having caught much,
complaining about late afternoon heat,
spitting tobacco into a white plastic bucket
empty of bait, a couple of their kids
will be torturing an overturned
stingray with a jack-knife,
watching it writhe and curl
as they jab its underside and draw away,
wary of a lash from its stinger,
and you feel like it's your heart,
but you don't know why or for how long
it will hurt, listening to waves crest and recede
among the creosote pilings that shudder
under the sway of your legs.

Michael Foran

The Garden

Just a morning spent expanding the garden
a corner shaded by tall sumac and maples
that led back to the swamp
and as she worked the new area
with a small trowel and a metal hand tool
a claw, the kind that looks like a four fingered hand
palm down, wretched fingers curled under
like the last time she held her mother's hand,
the turn of the dirt raising pieces of glass
a rusted can, charred wood and ash
then a soldier, dirt caked, olive green
molded in the prone position ready and taking aim
and as she scraped deeper and further
more soldiers, one sitting talking into a radio
another arm back, pin pulled, ready to throw a grenade
one missing a head, the body gouged
and after she cleaned each one with water
she placed them on a rock and thought
if she'd had the boy, he would be a man now and he might
have thanked her for finding lost toys,
his green army of men, even the one chewed by the dog.

Bill Garvey

Schizophrenic

for David

He could be charming
                        like the time at Applebee's
flirting with our waitress   as if
            she couldn't see   the hospital wristband
                        he hid awkwardly   and when he
wrote
            her number on a napkin
        as if he'd call   cup the receiver
                        muffle the random shrieks
did he think she'd fall
                        in love?
            plot his escape?
                        ride the rails to Orlando?
                        breathe
The Salvation Army's tubercular wheeze?
                        he smiled in the car
            to let me know
                        he wasn't delusional—
        he winked
                        as he flipped through my CD's   I left
him
                        with other patients huddled
                        for a smoke   in my rearview
I watched him stomp
                        the cold
        from both feet   as Jagger wailed
                                                Shine A Light
I wish it had been me   who found him not the cops
        with their jars of Vicks
                        I wish I could have
            dumped his trash   bagged his clothes
                        found those photos of him
        waking to Rushmore   somewhere
in Wyoming
                        he snuck up on

41

                              a snoring buffalo
                steam rose
from its back like mist
                from a mountain
                         he held his hands palms-up
beneath its snorts

                                   as if it wouldn't wake

Margaret Gibson

Small Rain

Not quite awake, dozy in the way bees are
after fumbling the lilies,
and just loud enough for me to hear,
you say, "It's raining." And because
I used to love the sound of the rain
I drift back into remembering what,
hard of hearing, I can no longer hear,
wanting to start the day alive to rain
that shimmers in the window screens,
and streaks tree trunks lichen-green
then misty, as the morning
clears. Closing my eyes, I've listened
to rain on the roof for years,
as if my hearing it would always
continue, rain falling on stones,
on nests and nurse-logs; rain
slicking the coyote's fur and the silky
trillium, rain-stippled, nodding
on the shaded slope west of the house.
Beyond the window spatter now
I watch the cloudy borders of this quiet
storm, grateful for our life together
in the no-sound of the rain—
where it is nearly possible to believe
that we ourselves will continue,
and the Earth will, long after
it falls to one of us to close the other's eyes.

Benjamin Goluboff

Max Ernst Remembers Peggy Guggenheim's Housekeeping

Of course the actual keeping was done by others,
maids on soft feet, liveried servitors
gliding discreetly out of view,
but the quality of the service had been impeccable.

And while the beautiful Dorothea
was his alpha and omega, his all-in-all and all that,
the woman would leave her dishes in the sink,
her little implements of beauty immodestly on view.

It came back to Max from time to time
that during the years with Peggy,
his shirts were returned
from the posh Manhattan cleaner's
in trim little boxes lined with tissue paper
like presents ready to be opened.

Pat Hale

Clues from an Unlabeled Photograph

This could be an image
of my mother's childhood home,
a place I've never seen.

Two women sit side by side
deep in the shade
of the front porch.

A round-bellied little girl
in a white dress stands near the edge,
one hand on the railing.

Someone hemmed that dress.
Someone tied the dark sash
and brushed her short hair smooth.

Someone weeded the ground
under the lilacs and left the grass
wild at curbside.

Someone threw open
second-story windows,
but kept the parlor windows closed.

A residue of glue on the back
of an old black and white photograph:
My mother's house.

Pulled from an album.
Torn at one edge, a corner lost:
This could be my mother's house.

Shellie Harwood

Along the Way to Okay Market

You were the age I am now
when I walked with you to Okay Market,
hand in sweating hand.
You pulling me and the bent old cage cart
along the sidewalk that shimmered in heat
like a desert mirage we would never ever reach.
Your pockets bulged with fresh clipped coupons:
15 cents off Prell shampoo, buy one Jiffy cornbread,
get the other not quite free.
Campbell's soup, ten for a dollar,
macaroni, four for the price of three.
Please don't use them, I begged with cheeks flushed
hot in scarlet horror. Pay real money instead.
But you spread them across the counter
like a royal flush, sure of a winning hand.
The line behind grew restless, shifting weight, flushed babies,
and broken patience from hip to hip and back.
And the lady said, no, this one expired already,
this one, this one, this and that one, too.
You wiped your eyes with wadded Kleenex
while I bent my head low under a veil of stringy bangs
and shame.
You were my age now when you counted nickels
out from a zippered coin pouch, said never mind
to candy corn and Jergen's lotion, sent me down the aisles
to put them back again.
You were the age I am, pulling the cart home uphill.
Did you see me open my fist and let the coupons flutter
into the Okay's parking lot puddle,
see me leave them floating like colored boats
half-off and sinking? Do you see me now,
owning my shame, never hungry, never wanting?
Wanting only you, so long past expiration.
My own date, print too small to read,
expiring soon.

Shellie Harwood

A Torrent of Sparrows

Songbirds plummeting.
In Colorado, swallows in the dirt, by the dozens,
across the White Sands Missile Range, south in New Mexico,
on up the west coast in Oregon forests,
along the east coast, dropping on the shore.

Everywhere, the whisper of songbird mortality.
Absence of avian chorus,
the silent stratosphere.
A torrent of sparrows.

Deep in Connecticut, the New World Warbler falls,
the rusty blackbird, Indigo Bunting.
Piping Plover keening with the Purple Martin
for smoked-choked skies, the marshes stolen,
and wetlands, lost.

I know you know this:
songbirds are humanity's messengers,
winging World War warnings,
harbingers of loss in coal mines,
singing on of the world off balance, on and on.

I think of all creatures slight of bone, of lung, of wingspan,
the toll on the sentinel; the unheard trill of something amiss.
I think of living, gasping things
felled by the cold snaps, the raging firestorms,
by the violent squalls of us.

And of the slaughtered songs, the murdered murmurations,
the heads we hang in shame.

Ruth Hoberman

My Husband, Having Listened to a Podcast, Tells Me

the marvel, apparently, is darkness. With so many stars
nights should gleam—brazen, neon. A dime-a-dozen,
stars are, he says: trillions, countless as sand-grains

but huge and fiery. So the primary marvel is darkness.
Curtain-drop, period, line-break.
No syntax without. So clouds can purple

or pale in shifting light. So bulbs can furl and fallow.
Darkness, he says, is the marvel, given how light
races toward us from stars, each vast—but far away

and rushing farther, space swelling faster
than scientists thought. So light lags, fails
to find us, leaves us alone in our emptiness,

with our single sun and our night—so scientists say,
he tells me, as I slip into sleep marveling
at our luck: the dark, this talk.

Ruth Hoberman

What the Bartender Said to the Horse

I used to play guitar like Joan Baez—long hair, sincere. *Let's face
it, Ruth,* my brother said, *your voice is still your voice, your face your face.*

Intrigued by a mirror at five, my granddaughter studies her self—
is she Petrarch on Laura, enumerating the beauties of her face?

Sharon Olds, her gray hair piled like a haystack slipping down a hill,
smiled into my seventy-ish eyes and said, *Write about your face.*

As hectic sparrows hop and peck at crumbs, a woman near me talks
to a friend about serums and Botox, creams and peels for her face.

In the mirror's lake, Plath wrote, a *terrible fish* will rise. I watch
as it kisses the woman it finds there: our lips at the water's surface.

Sallow, long-nosed, limp-haired: men called George Eliot ugly,
though she talked so well some loved her *great horse-face.*

All Paris loved *La belle inconnue,* her death mask on everyone's wall.
A suicide in the Seine, they explained, and kissed her plaster face.

What the bartender said to the horse, men say to women on the street:
Smile, they say, *whoever you are. Why the long face?*

Jennifer Randall Hotz

Sword Swallower

> *For K., who didn't make it; & for C., who hopefully will.*

I.
On the radio,
the story of a sword swallower who had died,
but not from what you'd think—
liver cancer delivered the final cut.
Surely the swords were fake, collapsible?
the interviewer asked.
No, they were real,
the reporter confirmed.

2.
At the lake where she told me,
a great blue heron glided past,
landed at the edge of the ice,
speared a silver fish—
oh the struggle as it slid down its gullet.
She apologized for ruining my vacation.
I cursed cancer for ruining her life.

3.
The danger:
on the journey through mouth, esophagus, on to stomach,
the unsparing metal cleaves aorta, heart, lungs.

The trick:
You have to embrace the fear,
the sword swallower once said,
Allow the esophagus to e x p a n d,
                    r e l a x,
   receive,
take into itself what could kill it.

4.
This day,
she swallows all that horrifies,

       petrifies,

        paralyzes,

takes into herself what could kill her—
chemo, yes, but also:

the sharp knowing

A.R. Johnson

Mourning Clothes

An empty cardinal's nest
Perched in the blackened rose canes

Like a rakish straw hat
With one feather still clinging to it.

A loose coat of ragged bark
Hanging from bent trunk and brittle limbs.

The size of the void left by the sole
Of a worn-out work boot in the frozen mud.

Icicles dangling like spangly earrings
From the rusted gutter rim,

And the pale and paper-thin skin of frost
Stretched over the bare bones of morning.

This is how we try on death
Every winter.

A.R. Johnson

Uccellini on the Piazza del Popolo

Like a charm of colorful birds dipping and turning against a winter
   sky,
Dozens of children in coats of red and yellow, blue and green,
Seen from above and at a distance,

Are racing in scattered patterns across the grey piazza.
Their teacher calls them, and they come swiftly together to settle on
   steps,
Young fledglings from a flurry of flight alighting.

I hear faint echoes of their laughter and chirping chatter
Coming back to me from old walls and empty spaces,
Causing me to remember

The black-and-white of ordered nuns in habits rigid with reasons
   why,
Their large, framed faces always too close, seeing into souls,
They said, as my guilt took flight.

Jason Kahler

How We Go

I'll get cancer. It ends us all, given enough time.
The folding and refolding of the grave, a body
eating a body. Already,
up and down my spine, the small cushions between bones
wither. Trace their failures between my shoulders
like an asp.
   The price of every snowhill,
every sled, toboggan, tube, shovel and tray I rode down
between unforgiving trees.
I've grown used to the click of my knees
and the deepening of stairs. Bannisters like
parachutes. Steps like

prayers. And sugar sugar sugar all my doctor discusses
is sugar. Soda is sugar. Beer is sugar. Bread is sugar.
So hungry
but everything is sugar.
The tendon in my left arm has snapped,
a defeated rubber strap curled beneath the skin
of my inner elbow. Don't ask me to move a sofa.
   I've hurt my back
putting on pants. My leg, too. Now
my hands look like my father's,
and the growing shine from my head.
His was his heart. This is how we go,
piece by piece, like forgetting.

Becky Kennedy

The Geese

When we went on without you,
the road was unchanged, welt of
late sun across the cars that
streamed off and on the highway
without you. We came down from
the hills, and the haulers and
carriers, high taillights like
roses in the well of dusk;

last sky, burying itself
at the other edge of dark
to which we too would return,
lit the silence. The flower
of a sound then, like a thing
I'd thought and not remembered:
the geese, and the bare music
pulling from them. The way we

want to live forever when
we can't go on. Dark falling
on itself then, the distance
closing, which is memory,
which is the only light, we
saw into the night as if
it were noon: the wide-mapped wings,
the geese glittering and gone.

Raphael Kosek

Poetry Lesson

After reading the poem, Nadia asks me, "is *lonely*
an abstraction?" and I say no, but loneliness is

and there is now always confusion because students
cannot tell a thing from something that modifies it

I've seen great blank canvases on a museum wall
brandishing emptiness and I understand how

nothing can be something so if I am *lonely*
as a cloud as I wander between abstractions

the cloud will whiten then melt into something
else, and when all the blue is gone, don't tell me

cloudy isn't a thing that covers the sky, don't
tell me *lonely* isn't hard and cold and simply

sad when you can't sleep and the night grows
longer, or your beloved cat dies or your husband

is away and you worry the plane will crash
and damn it, *lonely* sure as hell is a thing

when you can't remember a simple prayer
you've said all your life and you fear maybe

all your words will desert you one day and then
lonely will be the only thing you have.

Lawrence Leffel

The Retired Gondolier

He wakes from his afternoon nap
hears the gurgle of opal water under his bed
the whoof of pigeon wings in November air.
In wrinkled undershorts, he spreads green wooden shutters
like wings over evening's red tiled roofs, then inhales
puffs of cumulus that migrate a periwinkle sky.

Dressed for dinner, the retired gondolier
Descends the apartment's narrow stairs,
tests with his wingtipped toe the waters of the ancient street,
then tilts on sea legs with the roll of piazza brick.

At the restaurant he visits nearly every night
the dance his straight-backed chair at table makes.
He lifts a stemmed glass of house chianti, its melancholy
swirl the spray of his wife's hair when her train
to Milan rumbled away from now, then, and time itself.

"I detest the woman I've become with you," says his pasta,
tangled like hair as his fork spins.

The retired gondolier surveys the piazza and
its thousand lovers at dusk, as if in one embrace.
The old songs line up, take their turns
as he sips and chews, breaks the sturdy bread.

All his life he has abetted lovers washed in lilac light,
a welcome voyeur, the pilot with no particular place
to go, yet going.

Lemon ice softens in his spoon, the sweet and tart in balance.
He wonders where his wife has ended up.
Eventually, thick black coffee,
Then cigarette smoke deeply inhaled.

He thinks he sees her in the shadowed square,
her bold gait, her sassy breasts, and the mischief
in her conspiratorial smile, her eyes locked on his.

By the time he rises, the piazza is empty,
a lagoon of rolling brick that he navigates
without charts, cargo, or fare.
All about him, he thinks, men and women
stretch in the music of their nightclothes
secure as children in floating cribs.

V.P. Loggins

Out of the Distance

We used to go down to where
the tracks cut across the field,
and where we would set our ears
to the rails to see if we could tell
of oncoming trains. Some days
the sun would glint off the steel
as we laid our heads down, ears
to the warm metal. Danny always
swore he could hear it coming,
but I was never able to detect
the charging train. Then as if
by magic it would appear, dark
at first in the distance, growing
as it approached. We'd dare it
while it was well away to strike us,
dancing in defiance on the track,
but always at the last moment,
(or even before the last moment)
we'd step aside and save ourselves.
As it passed, a wild rush of wind
would blow our hair, while we
waved at the engineer, his whistle
wailing like a morning chanticleer.
Then we'd turn with our backs
to the rails and run wildly alive
across the wide eternity of the field.

George Looney

The Woman in Hopper's *Nighthawks*

Let's have a little fun, I hear a man say
as he takes a woman's hand and twirls her

to the kind of music that might be playing
in the stoic café in Hopper's *Nighthawks*

before they turn the corner and are gone, leaving
me snapping fingers to a tune suddenly

fallen silent, trying to hum it without knowing
where the melody should go. I want to

follow the dancers down some dark alley
where we'll alternate cutting in, the man and I,

while the woman giggles a concerto that might have
been scribbled down by a Mozart drunk enough

to hallucinate two masked ostriches waltzing
in sand crisscrossed by the sidling tracks of crabs

with more legs than any crab should have. When I dance
with the woman no doubt the alley will reverberate

with an unknown classical waltz and the cats
yowling amid the trash will harmonize

with the humming of the streetlights barely
a whisper in the dark of the alley, and everything

will seem to crescendo to a chord so passionate
and precise it will be as if light has become sound

and every woman in the world will want to
be the woman in Hopper's painting, who is,

of course, a variation of Josephine. Every woman
will want to be reading the inside of that book

of matches, believing what it promises
will mean she will never have to find herself

in a diner like this ever again. Rather,
the places she'll haunt will be elegant and filled

with a music that's clearly classical, a music
every patron will rise to from velvet-covered tables

to take the manicured hand of a woman or man
and start doing a waltz reminiscent of Venice,

and delicate birds, doves no doubt, will script such
words in fragrant air the meaning can't be missed.

Andy Macera

Second Divorce

You never finish anything, your mother said
when you told her, flashing back to

your childhood, the fuselage of a model
airplane on a table, the wings still in the box,

the brush from a lid of Elmer's Rubber Cement
resting next to the dried out jar; a pile of

books on a desk, their markers sticking out
like communion tongues; the basement floor

a failed factory of piecemeal projects built
from the steel and wood of an Erector Set

and Tinkertoys, abandoned in Saddington's
dark swamp of despair where the dreaded

creature of criticism can't grow, always distracted
by the novelty of stimulating thoughts of a

distant fantasy, high on exciting half-baked ideas,
daydreams spinning around like that carnival

ride you jumped off of before it stopped, eager to
eat elephant ears, to lick the powdered sugar off

your fingers, how they will wither away without
ever once knowing the feel of a finishing touch.

Paul Martin

Lovey

It was shy Lovey's mother that pulled him away
from us mocking kids onto the dance floor
at the wedding reception and showed him how
to hold his arms, relax his shoulders and step
a certain way until the stiffness slipped from him
and he learned on those Saturday nights
at the Sokol Hall and the Legion how to enter
the dance, moving smoothly as water,
slow ones, fast ones, anything old or new,
lovely women, kids and old babushkas coming alive
in his arms, dancers clearing a space
to watch him whirl and glide across the floor
in his pink shirt and blonde hair slicked back,
a spiral of light in our gray town, beautiful,
really, to see, though it felt too strange
to tell him so.

Ivy McCall

Simple Prose

Please love me
from a distance only
love me through a screen
where I can keep
the ugly parts
off-camera and unseen
love me through a mirror
love me through a lens
love me through a filter
that obscures
the great world's spin
love me like a record, baby
don't love the bruises
on my shins
don't love me like I'm sunlight
when I've got shadows for skin.
don't love me like the sinner,
when I am the sin.
love me like a pop star
you know you could never touch
like we could slow the spinning
when it's all just too damn much
love me through layers
of latex, rag and bone
don't love me like you'll make
of my body a home.
there is no shelter for you here
just an empty robin's nest
no respite from fear
just eggshells, unblessed.
this land is inhospitable
this model's past repose
so don't love me like a poem
when I am simple prose.

Rennie McQuilkin

On the Possibility of Renewal

Last night my son called to say he was cheered
for the first time in months. Maybe the world
was not ending, maybe tyranny was in retreat,
maybe war mongers would be upended abroad
and civil war avoided here, our own monger
manacled. "Listen," he said, "to the late reports."

I couldn't find the remote to tune in,
searched everywhere and in my distraction
felled a leaning tower of books, left them lying on
the floor, too much like the unburied dead
on the streets of a war-ravaged land.

This morning, in the unbooked space on my desk,
the remote, which did not fall with all around it,
turns up, a survivor. May it bring in good news.
I raise the bodies of knowledge sprawled on the floor
in their colorful jackets, turn back time,
try my best to imagine them as revelers at a wedding.

Nan Fitz-Hugh Meneely

The Hudson River at Coeymans, New York

Here, the river is kind
between freezes and floods.
It slows to nourish fields
sown down to its very edge,
affords a living to men
who load the barges
that hulk at the pier
like water mammals tamed.
At noon the laborers rest on its bank,
eat lunches their wives have packed
in the huddle of houses
across and below the River Road.
My grandfather, brickyard manager,
looks beyond them
to the turn of the river's tides
as he sips some noontime fortitude
from a silver flask.

Just south of the brickyard
the water slides below the hill
where my grandparents live
in a little Sears house well up
from the riverfront,
tucked between church
and the village doctor's home,
peaceful without and within.

In this house we are only loved.

The river threads itself
through a perfect day.
Mid-morning, we deliver
our granddad his sandwiches
and say hello to Henry Hughes,
who stops to walk us across a plank
to a half-laden barge

and holds the back of our shirts
as we lean to study the reasons
for eddies below.

And the river is the deepest secret
of a secret place at the back
of my grandparents' yard.
That's where the far house,
two raw pine rooms with a porch,
sits just short of the pitch
to the water's edge.

We play here, the riverbank one side
of our own small wilderness.
We breathe the musk
of the river's underside,
caught in its mystery, mindful
of stories of children carried away.
We are careful never to slip
toward the brambles and reeds
at its verge, scared to the perfect degree
of pleasurability.

At end of day, we sit in the comfort
my grandmother makes
on the playhouse porch,
waiting for wind off the water
to dry our faces, the backs of our necks.
When she persuades us we are tired
we travel her garden
back to the grownups' house
where we bathe
and dinner ends in time for Ed Sullivan's show.

The oldest child, I'm last to bed.
In the Fall when the trees are bare,
my sisters are finally still
and the street below my room
is as quiet as if the village had died,
I can hear the Hudson's gossiping.

I ease into sleep in the peace
of a house overlooking a river
that moves on ceaselessly
but, like our grandparents' cherishing,
is always there.

Erika Michael

What Happened to Jeki?
Or Dog as Metaphor of War

Let slip the dogs of war, they cried,
and so the many-headed Cerberus
flew off the fist—the "dog handlers
of Dachau" on command unleashed
their hounds to tear the prisoners to
bits, the red-eyed pack enraged with
spittled trickle on their gums and lips.

My Jeki—not a terror, but a terrier,
old snapshots show his white coat,
curly with some darker spots. I don't
know whether they were gray or brown.
He liked his liver, Mama said, and let
me put my fingers down his gullet.
When the peaceful dogs were called

to lick the poison bone, they lingered
fleetingly to warm a pillow, fetch
a stick, and then those baffled canines
gnawed the marrow from a stone.
My mother had to bring our Jeki to
a camp for Jewish dogs. Did he feel
abandoned, wondering where he'd

gone astray. Of course, it wasn't he,
but we who'd gone away—the roving
Jews aboard that bloody omnibus.
She's bending to his ear, and while
I thought I heard a fraught *good dog*
it might be that she said—*good God.*

Larry Narron

Lineage

I'm already halfway through
my own life when I ask you
to tell me again the story
of when you borrowed your sister's roller skates.
You used a key
to unlock the base plates
so you could refasten them,
metal wheels & all,
onto ¾-inch plywood.
Your father was there.
You held the vise
while he sawed the corners off one end
to make somewhat of a nose.
He found a leftover strip of carpet,
glued it down so you could ride
barefoot around the block.
This was San Diego, 1960.
That summer, your friends
heard rumors of surfers
who coveted even the sidewalk.
Neither of us could have known,
so many years after the fad
that swept your neighborhood
had faded, I'd find myself
pushing around in a schoolyard,
leaning toeside, trying to see
how sharply I could turn.
This was Escondido, 1997.

Sandra Salinas Newton

At a Party of Mourning Doves in Austin, Texas

A loft of doves rushes down to peck
At the seeds and broken *tostadas* thrown
Into the winter yard.

They clump together
                    like nervous girls
at a *quinceañera*
Bodies hot and trembling
With perilous anticipation.

The doves cannot stand still
But stamp their lightly taloned feet
And sing soft melodies to each other
While gulping down the charity
In frosty air.

Without strategy or tactic
They feed and worry;
                one or two *duennas*
                lookouts
                for the murdering cats
                who prowl this yard.

When the feast is over
Only one will have fallen
Caught in claws
Devoured, not unlike
                the innocent beauty
                who succumbs
                astonished
                to the fastest boy
While the rest
Complacent and stuffed
Fly home
Completely unaware.

Eugene O'Connor

Sewing Machine

In 1957 my aunt got
a brand-new Singer Slant-o-matic.
My mother helped her as she began
to work it out: simple stitches
at first, patterns
for dishtowels and aprons.

The lessons taking over,
my aunt forgot to take her pills
and later, just before supper
for our family at her house,
the darkness fell—a seizure.

She broke a dinner plate, still dazed
but coming back from where
she'd been, from that dark place
I first learned about when I was eight:
a life suddenly unraveling,
its colored threads gone slack and dull.

Maybe she could mend
the broken plate, the Singer's
clever needle whirring up and down
to sew it back together.

Maybe she could sew
her wings of flesh back on
and fly far above
the midnight drunks, the blackened eye,

the scramble
of crumbs and broken china
on a table.

Glenn Pape

My Wife Goes to Palm Springs with Her Book Club

When you return,
I'm sure you'll notice
that the basement smells like piss,
the coffee pot sits blackened
and ruined on the stovetop,

one stale cracker
and a stiff white sock
lie like fallen soldiers
on the dining room table.
When you return,

I hope you'll understand
there was never any cause for alarm.
The house was never about to burn down,
and the piss in the basement
is the dog's, not mine.

You'll find me waiting exactly
where I'm meant to be—lying on the couch,
an unfinished crossword littering the floor,
a melted cube and a whiff of Bourbon
tainting the tumbler balanced on my belly.

I'm drifting off slowly,
eyes half closed,
trying to reach
an agreement with the world.
It's Saturday at 5 p.m.

I could see twilight dancing
through the blinds, scattering flecks
of yellow gold across the walls.
Instead, all I see is one more day
dissolving into gray without you.

Matt Pasca

the heart gregorian

paper tulips taped to
        march windows, pumpkins

in september, snowflakes
        late november—all lies

premature & cartoonish
        like most elementary lessons—

seasons live in the body
the way sitting alone in a room

with my father was always mid-february
        our oil running out beneath

silence & ashtray smoke
my wife is early june: scattered leaf light

& hammock twine, the mosquito-less
yard & solstice rosebush riot

alarm clock intrusion is always march
the charcoal rain & soaked socks

ex-lovers october, favorite teachers
may clouds, good friends july nights of cups

sweating on patio benches & moaning
pylons in the bay   it's a january dawn

when no tree splits the sunrise over weeping
mountain temples glow through april dusk

after mud & obligation inter our better selves
saying the hard truthful thing is mid-november

when you pull trash cans to the curb
neck craned, eyeing flights to elsewhere

december flickers like a runway, stirs
new hope while september mourns

every failure to connect—my son rapping
alone at recess, his brother lost in imagined

brackets & red cards   we are misled
bullied by hallmark's impotent proofs

only love—in its dogged
demolition of parts—

holds us as a number
turns the page

Julia Morris Paul

For I Will Consider This File Cabinet
after Christopher Smart

For I will consider this file cabinet
for its metal-muscle. For its beige
stoicism. For the weight of what
towers on top of it, the to-do's and the
can't-do-without's. For its interior,
dark as a cathedral before the white-
haired widow sparks the first votive.
For its folders lined-up like soldiers.
For what those multi-colored folders
contain. For the ones that bulge with
old tax returns and the slim one
labeled, *Places to Go in Vermont*, a
single newspaper clipping slipped
inside. For here is my life as an adult:
receipts for capital improvements,
car titles, insurance forms. For here
is proof of my existence: birth and
marriage   certificates,   passport,
vaccination card. For one day my
children will rummage through and
find their report cards and essays
titled, *What I Did During My Summer
Vacation*. For who can know where
they've been without a paper trail?
For its humility and patience like that
of an English butler or the Buddha.
For its drawers that ache in and out.
For its bland interpretation of life;
a docent in a museum of scratches
and dents. For its lack of filigree
or bewilderment. For its rejection
of chaos. For not thirsting. For not
walking out. For not needing love.

Pit Pinegar

Holding Things Together

Sometimes,
when I am driving alone
on an open road,
I'm sure I have it right:
I travel with all that is lost
and all that is beautiful.
I hold it all, singing and
crying at the same time:
chantepleurer—only
the French could have
a name for it—
until I can't see the road,
must pull over,
let go of all
but the surface
I am traveling,

memory blocked,
past reduced—
just for the moment—
to what I can see
in my rear-view mirror.

David Radavich

Turning Russian

First they take our passports,
then our cell-phones,
copying our contacts
for their net of negation.

Then they make us strip
and take all our clothes.

We get new money—not much—
to spend on what they want.

We can no longer speak
like jailed birds.

We will pass into history
as a sieve. As smoke.

What will I still remember?
What will I know to sing?

We are cogs in their machine
that pounds everything
into the same grim paste.

I lie down in a bed not my own.

My face becomes foreign,
my body a ghost of the moon.

Charles Rafferty

A Love Poem of Sorts

This morning I threw a stone at a butterfly as it floated toward the purple hydrangea. Had I taken care while aiming, I'm certain I would have missed. Now its beauty is open to inspection, and I can rub away the powder of its yellow wings. After all these years, this is how I think of you if I think of you at all—my darling, my dead butterfly.

Gwen North Reiss

Hole in the Light

Giant when slant.
Shape of the thing

and its absence.
An isn't—in sight

and present. Noon
is a depressing time.

Too much supervision.
Evening—they make a garden

of wherever you are.
When a cloud passes

overhead, the ghostly ark
pulls a pond of dark through the air.

In the heat you'll cross
to their side of the street

to whatever of night lingers
between awnings

and concrete. In summer,
7 a.m., trees map

their columned tracery
on grass and street—

immaterial velvet
branch and leaf—not quite outline,

not quite grief.
And not entirely underneath.

Gwen North Reiss

To the Beet

Magenta bulb.
No onion scales.
A bleeding out

on the knife—
dense and darkest
sweet. How you dye

everything. Within
the sandpaper skin,
a core traced

with crescent ghosts.
Under the faucet, a pink
effusion ribbons

the sink. Sphere
and a rat tail,
all hair and spine at the base

of a planetary presence.
Your stalks are red, splayed
arrows with green leaves

arching over the ground
where you hid
a shock of incandescence

inside the drum. No one ate
beets at my house.
But I learned

on a cutting board
to open the root's
closed mouth,

finger its fluid edge,
stain my teeth,
break into the spilling ink.

George Ryan

At St. Hippolyte

North of Nimes, at St. Hippolyte-de-Caton,
an almost perfect rectangle of earth,
about an acre or so, lined by trees,
lay uncomfortably among the vineyards.
Its country plainness almost concealed
that its weeds and undergrowth were cut and cleared
and nothing was planted or allowed to grow.
I saw no sign of graves or foundations.
No stone walls, no iron gates, only silence.
Its emptiness among the rows of grapes
was a silent nod to memory.
What happened here? People with gentle minds
would not have lingered. I went every day,
if only to take in its eeriness.
I saw nobody, except a farmer once,
who stopped and watched and seemed about to run
until I spoke to him and he was polite
but in a hurry. I supposed he might
have thought I was an apparition
at first but discovered when I spoke that I
was only one of those foreign nuisances.

Peter Serchuk

At the Tule Elk Reserve

No fools for bad weather, Tule Elk live only
in California where the seasons keep them free
of a winter wardrobe and the political climate
spares them the hallucinations of poachers.
In return, they patrol their grasslands, mindful
to keep non-native shrubs on the run.

Coming up the western side of the Tamales Reserve,
where the trail looks down on the welcome mat
of the great Pacific, I see them on the ridge above;
the bull with his royal crown silhouetted against the sun
and nearby, the harem under his protection.

It's not long before he sees me too, an unwelcome intruder.
To get a better look, he moves forward to size me up;
a scrawny creature on two legs, not a quarter of his weight,
no match for a duel with his antler swords. He offers me
the choice: come forward like the other bulls he has broken
or turn back and leave him to his peace.

Of course how is he to know there is nothing to fear from me?
Armed only with curiosity, here I am the one unprotected,
the species more likely to be the hunted than the hunter.
And yet, the Tule do not hunt, they only protect,
model citizens of the world.

Slowly, I step back, step by step, let the bull know I am
not here to challenge but merely to observe, to lift my ears
to the reveille of his bugling; which is not a call to arms
but a reminder to the harem that August and September
are fine months for mating.

Alexandrina Sergio

I Think About Pasquale

An Italian immigrant
left with no speech and little mobility
following a stroke,
he was my husband's grandfather
known to me only through stories.
I see him through the eyes of a small boy,
his body curved on a daybed
in the family kitchen,
his thin bones warmed
by the window sun
his spirits sustained by
lingering aromas of bread and red sauce.

Then
bears little resemblance to
Now,
the Now of countless variations
on a theme of Elder Care,
the Now of
scheduled showers,
afternoon bingo,
bland dinners:
all quite logical
and useful
and necessary.

And yet...
my aging imagination
indulges a persistent fantasy,
a vision of solace and peace
in a family kitchen
perfumed by melanzane
where, when sight dims and steps falter,
I can know familiar comfort

while resting
on a daybed
in the sun
like Pasquale.

Susannah Sheffer

DMZ

At first they were not even letters but
sounds that made up a name, Dee em zee,
a political cabaret, which is to say
a collection of responses
to the world at the time. I saw it on
posters and ticket stubs before I saw it
in the newspaper: The *DMZ,*
which meant to me and therefore fixed
in my mind the feeling of entering a space
and standing quiet and singular next to the
adults. The sense of an interior,
coming into a dark bar from the daylight,
the effort to make something out of the
detritus around you. I knew the response but not
the origin, didn't understand that war or
the others, the rivers and rice paddies
or the kitchens and bedrooms throughout
our own country. I still don't know what a DMZ is,
not really. I don't know how to create a zone
of neutrality, where people agree to
hold off or hold back. I don't know
how people fight or stop fighting.
What is the zone in anyone's house or country—
that word *demarcation.* How it gets done.
You walk down the block in any July
and the door to the synagogue is open
so the men's chanting spills all the way out.
Another sense of interior, the fervor and cadences
and some sense of the way their throats
are holding something that goes all the way back
to a time when survival was not guaranteed. As it never is.
I did learn something about responding
but that doesn't mean I know how to make
the necessary space now. There are so many letters I
hold in my mouth.

Vivian Shipley

An Art Therapist Observes a Ukrainian Boy
Drawing a Picture of His Mother

Roman, other orphanage therapists try
to keep you from making friends
because they are afraid your despair
is contagious. Trying to weight you into
this new world, they feed you stones
labeled: *Agency, Insight, Strategies.*

I want to witness what you saw,
the unspeakable, in order to honor
your loss and help preserve memories
you must have of your mother:
her hands stained by peeling beets
for borscht; peeling potatoes
for pierogi; the burn you inhaled
from horseradish roots she grated.

Trained to know there's visual identity
for what has no words, I learned
that children who witnessed horrors
often focus on lighthearted images:
sunflowers or an orange striped cat
on a blue kitchen table. But for those
who confront their loss, tanks, drones,
explosions, their family's corpses
littering the garden or the doorstep,
the order in which they draw
traumatic episodes from their lives
is significant, starting with the most
frightening aspect, then polishing
details, never going back to the original.

I take notes of colors you use: first,
pavement, shaded in grey streaks left
by missiles longer than a school bus;
next, an outline of your sprawled mother

in black; then a red crayon to smear
a rivulet from her mouth. Stick legs
of neighbors step over her body,
followed by you, running to life,
straight lines overhead for planes
dropping teardrop bombs from the sky.

Roman, with no grave to visit,
no picture of her face to frame,
how will you ever mourn, accept
your mother's meaningless death?
I will not burn your memories
into ash to erase touch of her hands
or build a coffin for your heart.

To give you words to grieve,
if I can get you to use red to color
in hearts, the yellow and orange flames
from missiles for birthday candles,
you might begin to imagine a future
containing her loss as morning glory,
impossible to uproot, that intertwines
to flower into hope for a new life.
But, a bell rings and our art session is up.

Vivian Shipley

Cropped

I vowed I would never haunt anyone,
be a bother like May Milton
in Henri de Toulouse-Lautrec's
At the Moulin Rouge (1895).
While walking out of the frame, she
peers from the right edge, looking
not directly at me but slightly above
and beyond. What must be gaslight
shines up into her face, tilted backward
so light contours her nose, cheeks
and brows like I did to frighten cousins
on Halloween, holding a flashlight
below my chin. This painting must
hold the memory of being cropped,
its right side detached. With May Milton
cut off, there was no focal point—
Not the five-foot tall, Toulouse-Lautrec
in center backdrop. Not the dancer
La Goulue arranging her straw colored
hair in a topknot standing behind a table
where, oblivious to anyone else,
a swath of Parisian bohemians circle
shoulder to shoulder. A woman
with ghostly pallor sitting across from
the flaming red-orange hair of Jane Avril,
socializes with the three men in top hats.
Was it the artist or dealer who scissored
May Milton out of the picture? Perhaps
her shocked face, battery acid green,
made it hard to sell. I'm standing before
the reunited 1914 canvas, but resentment
constricts my lungs, petrifies shoulder
muscles at the attempt to extinguish
a whole person. Being cut is different
than pentimento, being painted over
where x-rays can reveal prior existence.

Am I haunted by knowing May Milton was
once eliminated or fear of my own erasure
where there will be no restoration?

Christopher Shipman

Elvis Impersonator

Only in the car—only leaving or arriving—
my father sang like Elvis.
Any stretch of road longer than a song,
the ghosts swarmed the streetlights. Trauma
tangled in the trees. Every corner
a corner where his sadness and his fear
huddled like orphan siblings around barrel fires
no one saw. First, in the rearview

I saw his green eyes drift toward mine
as he backed out of our gravel driveway; beyond
the windshield's cracked glass
a blue house growing smaller on its hill.

The radio already on, after a few practiced flicks
of the knob, he'd lift a scrap—
whatever slapdash pop hit suited him.
No matter what it was, he turned it into Elvis.
Because my mother loved Elvis.

I knew nothing haunted that house—
its path of loose gravel coughing dust. Deep blue
like a voice finding the King's baritone.
Alone like eyes in a mirror of trees.
I knew it like I knew his palm would lift
from the wheel. The sound of the slapped dash—
a gesture designed for his wife
to lend an ear. I'm in the back, searching

the rearview. There's my baby brother beside me.
Plump—his breath bubbling spit.
The radio cranked, the old man leans in.
Springsteen's "Pink Cadillac"
—*somebody tempting somebody.* Just like that,
his memory a spreading fire.

Decades later, I'm driving to pick up my mother
from the airport. My daughter asked
to ride along. The windows down, we blast
Lady Gaga. Soon enough I'm singing—slowing
down every word of "Poker Face"
to a blue baritone. Behind princess sunglasses,
somewhere drifting in the rearview,
my daughter's eyes searching for mine.

Joan Seliger Sidney

Shame

Once when I was twelve, Mom sent me
around the corner to the drugstore for her Kotex.
How I wanted to tell Mr. Borsuk, the pharmacist,
"It's for my mother, not for me," but shame
zipped my lips, which he must have read, as he
brown-bagged the box and handed me my change.
Once instead of fasting on Yom Kippur, Mom
sent me to the Italian meat market at Avenue P
beneath the El to buy the quarter-pound of ham
I refused to eat. "Suit yourself," she said, and
chewed her ham sandwich on buttered bread.
"When I was growing up in Poland, your grandma
let me eat 'qvetchadik'—that's the noise pigs make—
on wax paper in the street." Not on the High Holidays
I wanted to say but was ashamed for Mom. For Dad, too,
who, instead of praying at synagogue, worked
day and night at his Mariners' Suppliers Store
selling dungarees and underwear to Italian
sailors while the Andrea Doria docked.
One morning, brushing my hair before rushing
to high school, I stared at my profile in the mirror;
too ashamed to smile back at my bone mogul nose.
For elective surgery, not covered by insurance, my parents
paid the Park Avenue plastic surgeon.
                                        "Gilding
the lily," my homeroom teacher said, when I
returned from Easter vacation, my Roman nose
replaced by one that turned up at the tip.
What did I know sixty years ago, about the cost
of shame or whose shame mattered most?

Christopher Stewart

What Came After

This is not a story that tells itself in time.
It occurs in time, but is free of time
the way the body stores a memory: a scent
(the way his hands smelled like engine oil)
or a parcel of a phrase spoken to you
decades ago that you still hear.

Though they are owed an inestimable debt,
the boys who were with me in that house,
the ones who weathered that suffering season
when his carnal breath was hot on our slim necks
whispering his pleasures in our shame
know some things can never be reclaimed.
Our past became a charnel house of memory
shaping the bony present.

The years reveal a tally of losses:
recoiling from a lover's lips on our thighs,
begging for manhood in moments
when beauty and unencumbered desire
were offered freely. Again. And again.
The body's engine coughs, sputtering refusals.

We rejoined body and soul at the dented seams
by learning the raveled language of mercy.
Praise songs and doxologies of our own making.
Despite our still unsteady voices, rising
like wonders into the ashy rafters of time.

Steve Straight

Urinal

To illustrate the concept of personal space
I offered my class the example of the men's room urinal row.
No man, I said, seeing a single man standing at one,
would take either spot right next to him.
The women in the class laughed, the men nodded.

The next week a student said he would miss
an important class to appear in court—
because of your class. To test your theory, he said,
when I was in a bar in Westerly last Friday night
I saw one guy alone in the middle of the row and took
the urinal to his right. He pulled a knife on me
and still had it to my throat when the police came,
still cursing me and exclaiming his hetero-ness.

The rich history of urinals,
from ancient troughs to a patent in the 1860s,
from French *pissoirs* on city streets
to what Marcel Duchamp called "The Fountain,"
upside down and signed "R. Mutt" into art history,
includes my father discovering in Haiti
urinals filled with ice. He tried to melt
as much as he could, he told me,
as if dissolving some of Haiti's many ills.

Once in a pub in Galway,
as I stood before a ten-foot marble trough,
two men came in and took their places
on either side of me. I did not pull a knife
on either one of them,
partly because I had no knife,
but mostly because one was the U.S.
poet laureate, Robert Hass,

and the other the Nobel laureate
Czeslaw Milosz. No words were exchanged,
but we seemed to be writing a poem by committee,
one we would call "The Stream."

Maxine Susman

Sea Turtle, Cape Cod Bay

> *But as turtles head farther north to warmer waters that are the*
> *result of human-caused climate change, cold stunnings have become*
> *more frequent. —Turtle Island Restoration Project*

Cold-stunned on Great Hollow Beach
a 350-pound loggerhead barely stirs.
The crew from the Truro DPW
wrap him in a tarp, haul him to rescue

but experts at the Audubon can't save him,
vets at the Aquarium miles away
can't save him. In his dying
he reveals what it's taken to live,

head stained green from algae,
mollusks fringing the scutes of his shell,
carapace crusted with barnacles,
so much life clinging as he ebbs away.

Sea-obese, he had eased his bulk
through the water, thick jaw crushing
the shells of deep food. Now he drifts
in the wide bowl of his body.

He could have lived decades more.

Cindy Veach

Skillets, Galaxies, and a Snow Moon

I don't know what happened
       to the cast-iron skillets my father collected

             from thrift shops around Chicago—
rusted, in need of steel wool, olive oil, heat.

When I come across cast-iron sets
       in the Vermont Country Store catalog

             I turn the page. It's raining, gloomy
but there's a Snow Moon coming—

a welcome respite from the darkness.
       My father was overprotective, maybe paranoid—

       dead bolt, door chain, secret knock—
no place was safe. I was afraid to go anywhere alone,

afraid of my shadow. He left me
       before the discovery of a rare monster galaxy—

             a massive blaze of suns that spawned
in the early universe then died. Even now, its dark matter

looms in the cosmos, isolated,
       no longer birthing stars. If there is life after death

             what is this galaxy's fate?
I followed his instructions to a T—

and yet, his carbon, his dust.
       Will I ever know what happened

       to those skillets? Their constellation of crumbs,
congealed grease, droplets of condensation quivering.

Alinda Dickinson Wasner

Had Things Been Different

Had things been different.
I might have run off with him
As was my first inclination
But that would have meant
Leaving the children behind,
My book unfinished

And spring was in full bloom
The cottonwood spilling its seedlings
And all that "cotton" flying with the bad
Company of the willows, the fluff
Sticking to our eyes—

And maybe if the birch trees and alders
Hadn't been shedding
Or the oaks filling with staminate flowers
For the second time
And the grasses releasing so much pollen
We might not all have been
So completely miserable

I could have just disappeared
Mid-morning or evening
The dog in the yard the children
In the shadows, porch lights
Just coming on
And the seventeen-year cicadas
Ratcheting up their relentless refrains

Given the right circumstances
I suppose I might have been happier
The sunsets brighter
The days more exotic—

But bring me the book again
That I might reread it

Might find myself on a different page
Find him somewhere in an adjacent chapter
The corner turned over
My name still emblazoned
On the flyleaf of his heart

Jane O. Wayne

The Branch in Question

Night after night the pond
lets go of its moon
         to grieve in darkness,
and I'm at it again
in a place so narrow
         I have to look straight up
to find the sky.
For nearly a week, I have been
         waiting for the closed
daffodils in the vase to bloom.
Soon I will have to admit my failure,
         try something else—
walk away perhaps,
but what if loss takes hold,
         pulls me back
like metal filings
yearning for the north?
         Three days in a row,
the barred owl perched
in the empty tree
         near the kitchen window,
on the fourth day
broke its promise.
         A week later the branch
still waits like a vacant chair.
How long does absence last?

John Sibley Williams

Bad Water

It is almost morning somewhere
& on the wooden sign beneath

the sycamore only splinters
remain of what may once have been

an apology. At least, a truth. A history
of unforeign bodies still hanging

in the near newness of dawn
from the previous night's white

rage. Only then, the cutting down.
The bad water

still stretching along the edges
of town, sweetly

poisoning the wells our god-
fathers wet our lips with after

the fall. & feeding the deep roots
of the sycamore. & the stars

scattered by a closer light.
There is something terrible

beneath my tongue, even now,
that is not thirst. Or language.

Not even forgiveness hurts
the photos of the men

we've struggled decades not
to become. Not even the fire

from the burn barrel where
we burn our ghosts keeps

our ghosts in their place.
Somewhere, where it is almost

morning, the morning this time comes.
Ropeless, the tree. Bloodless, our drinking.

Katherine E. Young

On Merwin

how long it took as you tried and failed and
tried again to unstaple the word from the page
seeking its living essence rather than an inky simulacrum
through Provence through Hawa'ii through Pakistan
where you chronicled the baiting of the bears
each year my uncle gave me your book a new one
each year the words spilling across the page like
shells and mollusks and sea anemones of the blind
seer of Ambon who as you do mined the sorrows
of his life for beauty he writes too much said
my uncle sadly they take him for granted he
should just put back the punctuation I said
to myself each time each time I was mistaken

Katherine E. Young

Still Life with Jell-O

Farmville, Virginia

The becoming-house place where dragonflies
and tadpoles caught the morning sun became
a house: strangers live there now. The cedars
with their knobs and mossy fixtures decomposed;
fields of waist-high grass were mowed; the fencepost
where a ten-year-old argued politics
with God fell long ago. The motel changed hands
several times, though each morning they still
collect wet towels and throw away used soap.
The ranks of pipe at John's Equipment still march
beside the highway; bald tires still litter the woods.
The nursing home has sprouted two new wings,
but my old piano teacher, Miss Emily Clark,
still sits there eating Jell-O, for all I know.

James K. Zimmerman

House for Sale

the house next door is for sale
        it has been for a year
clean
      patient
             hopeful
      alone

           waiting
for a young expectant
      and expecting couple

who will fall in love
      with wide-plank
hardwood floors converging
          lazily at doors
that can't close fully
      from years of lead-
based paint

who will fall in love
      with windows   of wavy
bubbled glass and cracks
         where winter's
      bony fingers can creep in

and warps where breathy
      wetness will keep
them tightly closed
         in summer

the house next door
      is an old woman
lying passive in a creaky bed
      her dress of faded flowers
and sutured tears

waiting to die, waiting
       to be reborn, waiting
for someone to wake her
         with a kiss
throw the windows open
      let the dust drift out
let the sun
           crawl in again

CONNECTICUT POETRY SOCIETY
PRIZE WINNERS

Experimental Poetry Contest, 2022
Judge: Richard Deming

Winner
Brandon Kelley

This audio poem seeks to engage with the essay
"The Promise of American Poetry" by Bob Hicok.

Find the active link for this audio poem on the website
http://www.ctpoetry.net/experimental-poetry.html

About the Judge: Senior Lecturer in English and Director of Creative Writing at Yale University, Richard Deming is a poet, art critic, and theorist whose work explores the intersections of poetry, philosophy, and visual culture. His poetry collection *Let's Not Call It Consequence*, received the Norma Farber Award from the Poetry Society of America.

Connecticut Poetry Award, 2022
Judge: Terry Bohnhorst Blackhawk

1st Prize
Aaron Fischer
"Got My Mojo Working"

2nd Prize
Shellie Harwood
"What Bloomed in Dresden"

3rd Prize
Kathryn Jordan
"White Flag"

About the Judge: Terry Bohnhorst Blackhawk is Founder/Director Emerita of Detroit's InsideOut Literary Arts Project, a writers-in-residence program that encourages youth to think broadly, create bravely, and share their voices with the wider world. Her poetry collections include *Escape Artist,* winner of the 2002 John Ciardi Prize, and *One Less River.*

First Prize, Connecticut Poetry Award 2022

Aaron Fischer

Got My Mojo Working

> *On learning that Muddy Waters' house has been awarded landmark status*

Unsee the weather-warped plywood
nailed over the windows, loops and whorls
distinct as the tideline, the chains and padlock

shackling the front door, where someone
has twisted the heads off
the decorative flamingo silhouettes.

Unsee the green and brown glister
of beer bottles smashed on the stoop,
the stair-step pattern between

bricks where the mortar's leached away,
the red X posted by the city to warn
firefighters the building's unstable.

But all the masons and carpenters
on Chicago's south side, the roofers whistling shrilly
for another pallet of shingles, the plumber sweating

the new pipes, can only minister
to the visible, a redlined two-story with too few
windows in a dicey neighborhood,

a cockeyed pyramid on the roof, like a false
start on a minaret,
a narrow house the blues bought.

That's like mistaking music
for the instruments used to make it:
the piano and drum kit in the basement

rehearsal room, the double bass,
mic stands, amps, long runs of cable
duct-taped to the scarred linoleum.

Or the upright in the front parlor.
Or Muddy's guitars leaning against the sofa,
"The Hoss" taking pride of place,

the '53 Telecaster he bought new
and painted candy-apple red. It carried him
from Delta gutbucket and bottleneck,

from the "good moaning and trembling"
of the church, the wind-tousled kerosene lanterns
setting apart the Friday night fish fry

from the pre-electric dark.
It's what called the elders to him, before
they had a record spinning on the jukebox,

a song charting on the hit parade—
B.B. King and Chuck Berry, Buddy Guy and Otis Spann.
Little Walter, who transformed

the blues harp into a jazz sax.
And Muddy's pale, short-lived acolytes—
Johnny Winter, Mike Bloomfield, Paul Butterfield.

They all could hear the sweetness in his music
that broke into joy—the buoyant shuffle
of I Can't Be Satisfied,

Hoochie Coochie Man's strut and vamp.
And they sent their joyous racket
out into the world.

Second Prize, Connecticut Poetry Award 2022

Shellie Harwood

What Bloomed in Dresden

When the shriveled men feel need again
to invade another country
and the talk talk talk is tanks rolling in,
missiles launched, air raids, and nuclear options;
when the earth begins again to shudder,
I go to the cupboard and pull down the chipped and yellowed tin
where my people, mostly unknown to me,
left recipes copied in my grandmother's palsied hand,
pick a comfort card, any old card, and begin.

When I hear of refugees and mortar shells, artillery,
I begin to assemble Berniece's applesauce cake,
spiced with my childhood,
and I sift and sift, soak raisins on through the sirens,
while the shelling rocks the counters
five thousand counted miles away from me.
My arm spent from mixing, I pour brown batter
in the cracked glass pan, as all the women who share my blood
have poured it, secure it in its oven, wait for it to bubble and rise.

When I wait, I think of Ukraine, of Afghanistan,
of Vietnam, Iraq, and Normandy.
And I wonder what bloomed before bombs in Dresden,
what flies or crawls or claws its way out of Ukraine.

I ask the internet to show me the national bird
of Ukraine, the color of wings to watch for as it makes its frantic way
under the radar, out of choking skies.
Two birds are pictured, white stork and nightingale.
Which is it, then? I have no one to call in Kyiv to ask,
which creature flies for you?

When I hear that they have breached the border of Chernobyl zone,
when I am breaking from the massacre in Bucha,

I pull Berniece's cake from the oven, hold it hot and close
against me, carry it steaming outside where
there are still wild and hungry things.

I fill my own mouth first, in handfuls sticky with raisins
and soft fruit; crumbs fall like cardamon tears.
The rest, I crumble along the fence line
for the nightingale or the white stork.
Whichever might land here, gasping from invasion,
stumbling its way to me.

Third Prize, Connecticut Poetry Award 2022

Kathryn Jordan

White Flag

for Kirk, 2/1/60 - 9/11/20

I follow bike tire tracks into the marshes
where you lived your portion of life,
looking around before I leave the trail.

I don't want anyone to see me clambering
down the embankment, pickle weed
squishing under my Merrell boots.

Remember when I caught you smoking
pot at twelve? After fifty years, I realize
I must have yelled something about trust.

What you wrote is still in my scrapbook,
your elegant, penciled script slowly fading.
"Trust is when you say, 'I'll be out with

my friends at the disco. There won't be
any trouble.' Tell me what trust is tomorrow,
okay?" As if I knew. As if you didn't, from

the lack of it. Now I read a solemn poem
as a white bird appears and hovers above
in the wind, observing your last rites. Are

you with me as I begin to pour—as bits
of your femur, patella and clavicle swirl
out over the water and glitter like stars?

I want go back and hold the jolly baby
you were when you were my little brother.
But the gull is gone and the jar empty.

I search the rippled surface of the tidal
stream and find you drifting down, landing
softly on the sandy bottom, a white flag.

Vivian Shipley Contest, 2022
Judge: Charles Rafferty

1st Prize
Srinivas Mandavilli
"Blackouts"

2nd Prize
Rosa Lane
"Dents de Lion"

3rd Prize
Claire Scott
"Cold Bleak Lack Versus Spring Crocuses"

About the Judge: Charles Rafferty has published 15 collections of poetry—most recently *A Cluster of Noisy Planets* (BOA Editions, 2021). His poems have appeared in *The New Yorker, Oprah Magazine, Poetry Daily, Verse Daily, The Writer's Almanac with Garrison Keillor,* and in numerous other venues. He has also published collections of short stories and a novel. Currently, he co-directs the MFA program at Albertus Magnus College and teaches at the Westport Writers' Workshop.

First Prize, Vivian Shipley Award 2022

Srinivas Mandavilli

Blackouts

I played with a swan when bored, turning its long shiny steel throat, revealing the belly and there lay betel nut leaves, slake lime, clove and cardamom. In its silver eyes there was darkness. The windows were covered in newspapers painted black, and just before the sirens sounded, I would run to my neighbor's house. Rabindra sangeet always seem to play on a spool tape player. I was shy and seldom ate the okra boiled with rice. In the rising steam, they were always so soft, so moist, so green. Once I heard my parents talk about the naughty twin brothers from the neighborhood. They were last seen walking holding hands along train tracks. That week I grabbed onto a live wire, and remained quiet, unmoved, worrying everyone and a soothsayer was called to examine my hands. My best friend stopped coming over. Years later found that her father had passed away, poisoning himself using a rusted metal pin as a toothpick. I am latitudes away, but still look at where the soothsayer's finger had rested on each mound of my right palm following its lines to the wrist. I had not heard what he had told my parents and I retrace those lines again and again. They stretch across my body, all the way to my head, my feet. Sometimes, I trip over those lines. I am watching the ticking bright radium hands of a clock and can hear the mythical golden

bird yoked to horses
studded with pearls and parting
the weltering night

Second Prize, Vivian Shipley Award 2022

Rosa Lane

Dents de Lion

> *The tube uplifts a signal Bud*
> *And then a shouting Flower,—*
> *The Proclamation of the Suns*
> *That sepulture is o'er.*
> —Emily Dickinson, from 1519

Pappus, a dandelion
                    clock of seed,
          full halo

                              lunar puff. My parachute
                    a host
of soft bristles
                    impels me
miles

                    from my single parent
          wind—
blown. Fragments
                    of poetry
          carried

                              in the daily pocket
                    of my garden
dress, summer's
                    hands
          sweet

                              with dirt. Each fascicle
                    a bundle
of poems, vibrissae
                    suspended
          by vortex

                    that tiny eddy

of air, my bristled
tail wind, lands
my descent
to the common

meadow, or
to the sandy mortar
between walkway stones.
I am
the golden medallion

sun stippling
earth, I feather
a plume of stars. I am
leafy toothed
grown basil,

my serrated dents
de lion—
immortal, *called back*
relentless, I roar—
madden every single plot.

Third Prize, Vivian Shipley Award 2022

Claire Scott

Cold Bleak Lack Versus Spring Crocuses

Sweet Pea Journal sent an email accepting my poem
"Cold Bleak Lack," which I wrote while staring
at six orange vials and a bottle of vodka.

Did you know seventy percent of the universe
is made up of dark energy?

They want me to change "ODing on despair"
to "feeling slightly blue,"
and delete the first five stanzas.

And they want a more upbeat stanza to end the poem,
like *"something something something spring crocuses."*

Really? Who cares about crocuses when you are
careening over a cliff, no strawberry bush
to cling to on the way down.

Yes, you can take my heart of glass
and toss it on the floor. Ha!

They have no idea about scab-picking the past.
The slow seep of sorrow like a leak in the basement,
unnoticed until you slip-slide in murky memories.

A child wears a wool sweater in summer
to hide swelling bruises.

A girl walks beside a freeway
her backpack filled with favorite books.

Listen: the devil is tuning his fiddle.
Can you hear the recorded laughter
of the long dead?

Can you see the burst of yellow
as crocuses flame the snow?

Margaret Gibson Poet Laureate Poetry Award, 2023

for a poem on nature in a time of global climate crisis

Judge: Margaret Gibson

1st Prize
Jenevieve Carlyn Hughes
"Etude for Elephant"

2nd Prize
two poems tied for second prize
Jude Rittenhouse
"Breath"

Abu Bakr Sadiq
"Displacement Theory"

3rd Prize
Anne Hampford
"Morning Yoga with Fruit Bat"

About the Judge: Margaret Gibson was Poet Laureate of Connecticut from 2019-2022. She has thirteen books of poems from LSU Press, most recently *The Glass Globe*. Her new book, *Draw Me Without Boundaries*, will be released in 2024. Her awards include the Lamont Selection, Melville Kane Award, and the Connecticut Book Award for *One Body* (2008) and *The Glass Globe* (2022). She was a finalist for the National Book Award (1993) and the Poets' Prize (2016).

First Prize, Margaret Gibson Poet Laureate Poetry Award 2023

Jenevieve Carlyn Hughes

Étude for an Elephant

25 miles from Ivoryton, Connecticut

A hundred years ago, a piece of you
in nearly every parlor. Carols sung

over polished wood, rich-grained
rosewood sheen, veneer of ivory.
At school, an instrument whose shape
and sound were like a living creature,
confined inside the auditorium—

while down the hall, we learned what passed
for history and science. We studied
every subject but the wild. At first, I was
too small to reach the keys, my bench
was bolstered with a book: the Yellow Pages

were never any use to you, your trumpeting call
can be heard for miles on the savannah.

They say in twenty years, you'll disappear
from almost every habitat in Africa: heat rising
like a mirage. Drought, even in the wet season.
You who grieve and never forget,
while wrapping trunks around each other—

You are your own moonlight sonata,
You are yourself a grand piano.

The problem is your tusks
are worth their weight in gold, a liability
to which you are adapting. Yet if they grow short
or not at all, how will you still lift your young,
each time your herd stands vigil?

Even some ex-poachers have been trained
now to protect you, patrolling like kingfishers
over the acacias as the sun sets and rises.
Is it just about money in the end? Maybe
it's about something closer to redemption.

Take my generation: we were raised
on *Heal the World*, on *Ebony and Ivory*—

we learned to read sheet music as a harmony
of black & white. In class we practiced our études,
noting all the flats and sharps, but no one told us
about Black bodies forced to cross a continent,
hauling your white gold upon their backs.

We were children, putting baby teeth beneath
our pillows, never dreaming less than half
a century ago, just up the road, a company town
and factory went on processing your tusks.
Your trust in us must have been shaken.

The elephant in the room? The human being:
not always humane, nor even thinking.

The ivory trade, banned widely years ago
still goes on, illicit poaching. Antique
pianos can be bought and sold, commodities
without recrimination. If the funds from each
antique went to the elephants—

it could be instrumental. Grace notes on a past
still present, and still visceral.

All those memories of my childhood recitals:
if I could choose from any concert venue,
your watering hole is now the only lounge
I'd ever want to play. I would try to find
a common chord while you splash & bellow,

we could communicate like that. I'd ask
about your herd. You'd trumpet back.

Jude Rittenhouse

Breath

Outside my window, dust
dances in a field
across the road, rises and makes wind
visible as your breath
in cold morning air. Beyond this field,
blue Atlantic marries sky
at an invisible and infinite horizon. If you
and I could look
through a window and see
deep into galaxies and time, we might
glimpse Higgs field
and, beyond that, the still, silent
ocean. Not a drop
of water. Just a quantum
vacuum: the background state
of the universe. In this ocean, existence
appears as waves: oscillations
of energy. Planted close beside ocean:
Higgs field. A fertile place.
The origin of all fields, all particles
in our universe. Look
what has grown here:
you, me, stars, snakes, water, wheat,
whales, trees. All of us connected
through our roots in this field. Every
speck of dust of us
alive, aware—infused by the wind
blown from that ocean. Filled by that breath
which lifts us and sends us dancing.

Abu Bakr Sadiq

Displacement Theory

what matters now   is not that even the rivers
are gone   & what's left are twined trails
of white sand   i always knew   it would come
to this   it follows a natural course   when
too many lives cling to the same prayer   in the fight
to remain rooted   in their home   someone
has to leave   eventually   abandoned houses
become homes   to the ghosts of those who couldn't
make it across the border   the nights
open themselves to more darkness   some
of the people i love are living   a new life
within the walls of   refugee camps in dar es salaam
others are busy   undoing the threads of trauma
on the streets of yaounde   i know i should have
chosen to live   like an armless shadow
bleached against a wall   it is easier that way
at least   i wouldn't have to remember much
of the past   or what i've lost   i get to escape
the cruel hands of memory   unscathed   i learn
to draw maps   on seashores   with a knife's tip
i get to walk through the neighborhood   offering
salaam to everyone   pretending they're still here

Third Prize, Margaret Gibson Poet Laureate Poetry Award 2023

Anne Hampford

Morning Yoga With the Fruit Bat Living Under the Eave

As always, she arrives at sunup. Circles the house three times. Closer
    with each circuit. This morning, her wingwind on my cheek. Then,
that impossible landing—full speed to full stop, upside down. How easily
    she changes direction, works her angles and fur, ends one thing, begins
another, certain of how she fits into the given space. While I'm rooted
    to this balcony in a country that isn't mine. Mammalian like her but
too stiff to feel elegant or agile as I move through the poses. She knows
    I'm watching. Her dark eyes don't care. She yawns a cavern of sharp
teeth, spreads her fingered-wing, starts to lick slow strokes from forearm
    to dactyl. Tubular tongue methodic. Elbow and wrist articulate. No clumsy
in her fan and fold. I envy the way she loves her body, the way her mouth knows
    its own funk and heft. How she slicks away sweat and tension with spit
and ritual. Then, sleeps loose, wings wrapped tight, swaying in the breeze.
    While I practice being a dolphin, a tree, an eagle. Something other than me.

Christine Beck

Reviews of Two Books by Connecticut Poets

The Unwalled City, **Robert Cording**

The title of Robert Cording's new book, *In the Unwalled City* (Slant Books, 2022), references Epicurus, who said that when it comes to death, we all live in an unwalled city. In poetry and prose, Cording inhabits the world of grief after the death of Daniel, his thirty-one-year-old son, who died after an accidental overdose of the pain killers which failed to relieve his back pain.

Written three years after Daniel's death, Cording, a retired professor from The College of the Holy Cross, invites philosophers and poets to both console and challenge him. He ruminates on Wordsworth's poem, "We are seven," in which a child counts her family as whole, even though two are in heaven. Cording admits that when asked how many children he has, he says three, although they now have become two. He finds objects which echo the contradiction of Daniel. For Cording, he is both here and not here. For example, Cording and his wife have placed a pottery votive candleholder fashioned like a Scandinavian church and a photo of Daniel in the dining room. "Neither of us think the little church houses our son's spirit….But now I visit it when I take a break from reading or writing, when a wash load needs to be moved to the dryer, when I make a cup of tea."

Cording's acceptance of his own grief and his desire to allow Daniel to live on the page resonate deeply. He uses prose to explain and poetry to explore his feelings. Together, they teeter back and forth in spiritual meditation on the loss of a son.

Affirmation, Steve Straight

College professor Steve Straight's book of poetry, *Affirmation* (Grayson Books 2022), displays his reverence for all of nature's creatures. "Telling the Bees," imagines a hive of bees in mourning for the death of the world. "Darner" finds the poet painstakingly freeing a dragonfly from a spider's web. And in "A Murder Question," the poet notices crows consumed with bitter cawing. Upon investigation, he discovers they are mourning one of their own, dead on the ground. As the poet gently buries the dead one:

> the crows gather in the maples nearby,
> softly keening now, witnessing my respects.

Straight widens his net to cast an ironic glance at many subjects, including his students who don't know when the Declaration of Independence was written or any facts about Gandhi. "hope/no hope" is his refrain.

His ending poem, "Affirmation," contains this epigraph:

> Note: This is intended as an oral poem. The speaker
> should improvise specific details of setting and actions.

It's a fill-in-the blank poem in which the reader can modify verses to earn the refrain: "We live in a beautiful, harmonious world / without war, or pestilence, or famine."

This is a fitting ending to a delightful compilation, the recent winner of the 2023 William Meredith Award in Poetry.

Connecticut Poetry Society Contests

The Connecticut Poetry Society offers several annual poetry contests, two of which are open only to Connecticut residents.

CPS board members are not eligible to enter contests.

Contest Winners must wait a year before entering again.

CONNECTICUT POETRY AWARD

In honor of Connecticut Poetry Society founders,
Wallace Winchell, Ben Brodine, and Joseph Brodinsky

Open to all poets
Opens: April 1
Deadline: May 31

Fee $15 for up to 3 unpublished poems, any form, 80-line limit
Prizes: 1st – $400; 2nd – $100; 3rd – $50

Winning poems will be published in *Connecticut River Review* and posted on the Connecticut Poetry Society website.

Winners receive a free, two-year membership in the Connecticut Poetry Society.

Simultaneous submissions are acceptable; however, please notify us immediately upon acceptance elsewhere.

Electronic Submissions Only
Submit at: www.connecticutriverreview.submittable.com.

Submit up to three previously unpublished poems in one document, no more than one poem per page; 80-line limit. No contact info on poems (contact information will be requested separately via Submittable).

We do not accept work that was created—entirely or partially—with AI software.

Guidelines are available on the CPS website: www.ctpoetry.net

VIVIAN SHIPLEY POETRY AWARD

Open to all poets
Opens: August 1
Deadline: September 30

Fee $15 for up to 3 unpublished poems, any form, 80-line limit
Prizes: 1st – $1,000; 2nd – $100; 3rd – $50

Winning poems will be published in *Connecticut River Review* and posted on the Connecticut Poetry Society website.

Winners receive a free, two-year membership in the Connecticut Poetry Society.

Simultaneous submissions are acceptable; however, please notify us immediately upon acceptance elsewhere.

Electronic Submissions Only
Submit at: www.connecticutriverreview.submittable.com.

Submit up to three previously unpublished poems in one document, no more than one poem per page; 80-line limit. No contact info on poems (contact information will be requested separately via Submittable).

We do not accept work that was created—entirely or partially—with AI software.

Guidelines are available on the CPS website: www.ctpoetry.net

NUTMEG POETRY AWARD

Open to Connecticut poets only
Opens: December 1
Deadline: January 31

Fee: Members of CPS may enter this contest without paying a fee; for non-members the fee is $10.

Prizes: 1st – $200; 2nd – $100; 3rd – $50

Winning poems will be posted on the Connecticut Poetry Society website.

Winners receive a free, two-year membership in the Connecticut Poetry Society.

Simultaneous submissions are acceptable; however, please notify us immediately upon acceptance elsewhere.

Electronic Submissions Only
Submit at: www.connecticutriverreview.submittable.com.

Submit up to three previously unpublished poems, in one document, no more than one poem per page; 80-line limit. No contact info on poems (contact information will be requested separately via Submittable).

We do not accept work that was created—entirely or partially—with AI software.

Guidelines are available on the CPS website: www.ctpoetry.net

LYNN DECARO POETRY COMPETITION

In memory of Lynn DeCaro, a promising young Connecticut Poetry Society
member who died of leukemia in 1986

Open to Connecticut student poets in grades 9-12
Opens: January 1
Deadline: March 15

Prizes: 1st – $150; 2nd – $100; 3rd – $50

No fee for up to 3 unpublished poems, 40-line limit

Winning poems will be posted on the Connecticut Poetry Society
website. Winners receive a free, two-year membership in the
Connecticut Poetry Society.

Simultaneous submissions are acceptable; however, please notify us
immediately upon acceptance elsewhere.

Electronic Submissions Only
Submit at: www.connecticutriverreview.submittable.com.

Submit up to three previously unpublished poems, in one document,
no more than one poem per page. No contact info on poems (contact
information will be requested separately via Submittable).

We do not accept work that was created—entirely or partially—with
AI software.

Guidelines are available on the CPS website: www.ctpoetry.net

EXPERIMENTAL POETRY CONTEST

Open to all poets

Opens: June 15
Deadline: July 31

Fee $15 for up to 3 unpublished poems
First Prize is $1,000
Up to four finalists will also be identified.

Winning poem will be published in *Connecticut River Review*
And posted on the Connecticut Poetry Society website.

Winners receive a free, two-year membership
in the Connecticut Poetry Society.

Submit up to three poems; text, audio and video files are acceptable.
Submissions may include poems composed using
1) an entirely new form;
2) an existing form that is considered experimental; or
3) a radical subversion of a traditional form.

No identifying information should go on the file (contact information
will be requested separately via Submittable).

Simultaneous submissions are acceptable; however, please notify us
immediately upon acceptance elsewhere.

Electronic Submissions Only
Submit at: www.connecticutriverreview.submittable.com.

We do not accept work that was created—entirely or partially—with
AI software.

Guidelines are available on the CPS website: www.ctpoetry.net

CONTRIBUTOR NOTES

Connecticut River Review
extends its sincere appreciation
to all its contributors.

Dennis Barone is the editor of *Garnet Poems: An Anthology of Connecticut Poetry Since 1776*, author of *A Field Guide to the Rehearsal*, and Professor Emeritus in English at the University of Saint Joseph.

Christine Beck holds an MFA from Southern Connecticut State University and is the author of *Blinding Light*; *I'm Dating Myself*; *Stirred, Not Shaken*, and a book of poetry and prompts called *Beneath the Steps: A Writing Guide for 12-Step Recovery*. Beck is a former president of the Connecticut Poetry Society and was Poet Laureate of the town of West Hartford, CT from 2015-2017. www.ChristineBeck.net

Maria Berardi's poems have appeared online, in print, in university literary journals, meditation magazines, newspapers, and art galleries. Her first book, *Cassandra Gifts*, was published in 2013 by Turkey Buzzard Press, and she is finishing her second, *Pagan*. She lives in Fort Collins, Colorado, at the foot of the Rocky Mountains. Her process is one of listening for transmissions and trying to catch them on paper before they dissipate: the glimpse, the complicated knowledge. www.maria-berardi.com

Tiffany Bergin was born in Hong Kong, grew up in the United States, and received her PhD in Criminology from the University of Cambridge in the United Kingdom. She currently works as a criminologist in New York City. Her creative writing has appeared in *Quarter After Eight* and *The Mays 17*.

paul Bluestein is a physician (done practicing) and a blues musician (still practicing). He lives in Connecticut near a beach where he finds quiet time to think about the past and wonder about the future. In addition to poems and short stories that have appeared in a wide variety of online and print publications, he has had two books of poetry published: *Time Passages* in 2020 and *Fade to Black* in 2021.

John J. Brugaletta is a Professor Emeritus at California State University, Fullerton. He has published his poems in 94 venues, some of which are *Ekphrasis, Extreme Formal Poems, Image, Pennsylvania Literary Journal* and *The Random House Treasury of Light Verse*. He has also published eleven volumes of his poetry.

Anne Champion is the author of *She Saints & Holy Profanities* (Quarterly West), *The Good Girl is Always a Ghost* (Black Lawrence Press), *Book of Levitations* (Trembling Pillow Press), *Reluctant Mistress* (Gold Wake Press), and *The Dark Length Home* (Noctuary Press). Her work appears in *Prairie Schooner, Crab Orchard Review, Salamander, PANK Magazine,* and elsewhere. She was 2009 Academy of American Poets Prize recipient, 2016 Best of the Net winner, and Barbara Deming Memorial Grant recipient.

Robert Cording's tenth and newest book is *In the Unwalled City* (Slant, 2022). New works are out or forthcoming in *Image, The Sun, Southern Review, New Ohio Review, Poetry Northwest,* and *The Common.* One of Cording's poems was published in the newest Pushcart Anthology.

Mark Cox teaches in the Department of Creative Writing at UNC Wilmington and in the Vermont College MFA Program. Recent work has appeared in *32 Poems, The Greensboro Review,* and *New Ohio Review.* His most recent books are *Readiness* (prose poems, 2018) and *Sorrow Bread: Poems 1984-2015.*

Dallas Crow is a high school English and photography teacher in Minnesota. His work has recently appeared in *Arkansas Review, Florida Review, Louisiana Literature, RHINO, Salamander,* and *Tar River Poetry.* His chapbook, *Small, Imperfect Paradise,* is available from Parallel Press.

John Cullen graduated from SUNY Geneseo and worked in the entertainment business booking rock bands, a clown troupe, and an R-rated magician. Recently he has had work published in *American Journal of Poetry, The MacGuffin, Harpur Palate, North Dakota Quarterly,* and *New York Quarterly.* His chapbook, *Town Crazy,* is available from Slipstream Press. His piece "Almost There" won the 52nd New Millennium Award for Poetry.

Patrick Daly lives in Menlo Park, California. His poem "Words" was a 2015 poem of the year in the *New Statesman.* His work has received honorable mention for the Pushcart Prize. He has published poetry recently in several anthologies including *The Place that Inhabits Us* and *America, We Call Your Name.* His chapbook *Playing with Fire* won the

Abby Niebauer Memorial Prize. His first full-length collection is *Grief and Horses* (Broadstone Press 2021).

Jim Daniels' latest poetry collections include *Gun/Shy* (Wayne State University Press) and two chapbooks, *The Human Engine at Dawn* (Wolfson Press) and the forthcoming *Comment Card* (Carnegie Mellon University Press). His new fiction collection, *The Luck of the Fall* (Michigan State University Press) is also forthcoming. A native of Detroit, he lives in Pittsburgh and teaches in the Alma College low-residency MFA program.

Jim Davis is a painter, poet, and an international semi-professional football player. He's a graduate of Harvard University, Northwestern University, and Knox College. His work has appeared in *Poetry Daily*, *Bellevue Literary Review*, *Harpur Palate*, *The Harvard Crimson*, *Portland Review*, *RHINO*, *Midwest Quarterly*, and *California Journal of Poetics*, among others. Twitter @JimDavisArt   Instagram @JimDavis.Artist

Emma DeNaples was born in New Haven, near midnight on October 22nd, 2000, which means, according to different sources, she doesn't know much about why she writes, but she does know that she has to, and that she wants to. She loves the world, even when it is harsh and fungal and fearsome, and she hopes her poetry reflects that.

Jeanine DeRusha teaches English at Manchester Community College in Connecticut. She holds an MFA in poetry from the University of Washington and has been published in several literary journals, including *Puerto del Sol*, *American Literary Review*, *Crab Orchard Review*, *Faultline*, and *The Seattle Review*.

Andrea Janelle Dickens is originally from the Blue Ridge Mountains and now lives in the Sonoran Desert, where she resides among the sunshine and saguaro cacti. Her work has appeared in *New South*, *Ruminate*, and *The Wayfarer*, among others. When not writing poems, she's making pottery in her ceramics studio or tending hives of bees.

Chase Dimock lives in Los Angeles in a four-person household, including a human partner, a Cavalier King Charles Spaniel companion, and a four-foot-tall statue of Slimer from Ghostbusters. He serves as the Managing Editor of *As It Ought To Be Magazine* and makes his living teaching literature and writing. His debut book of poetry, *Sentinel Species*, came out in 2020 from Stubborn Mule Press. www.chasedimock.com

Dante Di Stefano is the author of four poetry collections: *Midwhistle* (2023), *Lullaby with Incendiary Device* (2022), *Ill Angels* (2019), and *Love Is a Stone Endlessly in Flight* (2016). He is the co-editor of the anthology *Misrepresented People* (2018). He lives in Endwell, New York with his wife, Christina, their children, Dante Jr. and Luciana, and their goldendoodle, Sunny.

Sara Ries Dziekonski is the co-founder of Poetry Midwives Editing Services. Her first book, *Come In, We're Open*, won the 2009 Stevens Poetry Manuscript Competition. Her chapbooks include *Snow Angels on the Living Room Floor* (Finishing Line Press, 2018) and *Marrying Maracuyá* (Main Street Rag, 2021), which won the Cathy Smith Bowers Chapbook Competition. Her poems have appeared in *American Life in Poetry*, *SWWIM Every Day*, and *2River View*, among others.

Kathleen Ellis' book, *Body of Evidence*, won the 2022 Grayson Books poetry award. Other collections include *Outer-Body Travel* and *Narrow River to the North*. Her poems have appeared in *The Café Review*, *A Dangerous New World: Maine Voices on the Climate Crisis*, and *Enough!: Poems of Resistance and Protest*. Ellis has received the Pablo Neruda Prize and fellowships from the National Endowment for the Arts and the Maine Arts Commission. She teaches poetry at the University of Maine.

David Epstein, Ph.D. has lived in Connecticut since 2000. He repairs old buildings and likes racing small sailboats. Father of three, he won three poetry prizes in 2021. His works have appeared in *New Square* and *Olney Magazine* online. Recent poetry publications include *Marsh Hawk Review* and *The Bellingham Review*. He is a Board Member of the Hartford Friends and Enemies of Wallace Stevens.

James Finnegan has published poems in *Ploughshares*, *Poetry Northwest*, *The Southern Review*, *The Virginia Quarterly Review*, as well as in the anthologies: *Good Poems: American Places* edited by Garrison Keillor, *Laureates of Connecticut*, *Shadows of Unfinished Things*, *Imagining Vesalius*, *Waking Up to the Earth*, and *Walkers in the City*. For a decade he served as president of the Friends & Enemies of Wallace Stevens (stevenspoetry.org). He posts aphoristic ars poetica on the blog ursprache: https://ursprache.blogspot.com/

Aaron Fischer worked for 40 years as a print and online editor. He won the 2020 *Prime Number Magazine* poetry contest, as well as the Top Sonnet award from the Maria W. Faust Sonnet Contest for 2019 and 2021. Kelsay Books is publishing *My Shabby Afterlife*, a collection of poems.

Michael Foran is from Ware, Massachusetts, and teaches literature classes at Holyoke Community College. Some of his poems have been published in *Proud to Be: Writing by American Warriors, Driftwood Press, Ocotillo Review, Blood Tree Literature*, and *Medmic*. He earned an MFA from Goddard College. A United States Army veteran, he served as an infantry fire team leader with the 82nd Airborne Division. mforan@hcc.edu.

Bill Garvey's poetry has been published or is forthcoming in *Rattle, Cimarron Review, Nixes Mate Review, New Verse News, Margie, 5AM,* and others. He grew up in Springfield, Massachusetts, home of Doctor Seuss and the Basketball Hall of Fame. His MFA in Poetry is from New England College. Garvey is a dual citizen of Canada and the United States. He and his wife, Jean, live in Toronto, Ontario and Hacketts Cove, Nova Scotia for equal parts of the year.

Margaret Gibson was Poet Laureate of Connecticut from 2019-2022. She has thirteen books of poems from LSU Press, most recently *The Glass Globe*. Her new book, *Draw Me Without Boundaries*, will be released in 2024. Her awards include the Lamont Selection, Melville Kane Award, and the Connecticut Book Award for *One Body* (2008) and *The Glass Globe* (2022). She was a finalist for the National Book Award (1993) and the Poets' Prize (2016).

Benjamin Goluboff is the author of *Ho Chi Minh: A Speculative Life in Verse* and *Biking Englewood: An Essay on the White Gaze*, both from Urban Farmhouse Press. Goluboff teaches at Lake Forest College. His work is easily found on the Internet.

Pat Hale is the author of *Seeing Them with My Eyes Closed*, and *Composition and Flight*. Her work appears in many journals and is anthologized in *Forgotten Women, Waking Up to the Earth: Connecticut Poets in a Time of Global Climate Crisis*, and elsewhere. She has been awarded CALYX's Lois Cranston Memorial Poetry Prize, the Sunken Garden Poetry Prize, and first prize in the Al Savard Poetry Competition. She lives in Connecticut.

Anne Hampford calls Connecticut home, but she is currently spending time on the coast of Ecuador. Her poems have appeared in Terrain.org, *Crab Creek Review* (Finalist for their 2020 Annual Poetry Prize), *Naugatuck River Review, Connecticut River Review*, and *Dogwood Journal*. Her chapbook, *Everywhere Is North*, was published in October 2021.

Shellie Harwood's poetry appears in *TulipTree Review, Oberon, Mudfish22, Sixfold*, and *Montreal Poetry Prize Anthology*. She won the 2022 Nutmeg Poetry Award for her poem, "Afterswarm", and 2nd Prize in the Connecticut Poetry Award for "What Bloomed in Dresden". The title poem of Harwood's chapbook, *With My Sister, in a Tornado Warning*, was awarded the 2021 Oberon Herbert Poetry Prize. Her new chapbook, *Sleepwalker's Guide to Grieving*, was released in May 2023. She lives in Connecticut.

Ruth Hoberman lives in Newtonville, Massachusetts. Her poems have appeared most recently in *EcoTheo Review, Constellations, Ibbetson Street, West Trestle Review*, and *RHINO*. She retired in 2015 from the English department at Eastern Illinois University.

Jennifer Randall Hotz, a poet perpetually delighted by words, rhythm, and music, lives in coastal Virginia. She received an M.A. in English from San José State University and is looking forward to seeing her work published in various journals, including *Burningword Literary Journal*.

Jenevieve Carlyn Hughes lives near the Long Island Sound, a stone's throw from a railway line and two miles from a nature preserve with acres of coastal forest, sand dunes, and salt marsh. Her poems have been widely published, including the anthology, *In the Garden: Community Storytelling on Food, Ecology, & Place* (Torrey House, 2022).

Currently a writer for cultural organizations, she previously taught history and humanities for university students.

A.R. Johnson is a poet cum businessman in the tradition of Wallace Stevens, Dana Gioia, and Ted Kooser. Largely self-taught in poetry, he is a seven-time invited contributor to the Sewanee Writers' Conference, and his poems have appeared in *The New York Times*, The *Cortland Review*, *The Wisconsin Review*, and other publications. He lives and works in Tennessee.

Kathryn Jordan is a retired choral music teacher from Berkeley, California. Recipient of the San Miguel de Allende Writers Conference Poetry Prize and the Sidney Lanier Poetry Award, Jordan's poems have also earned Honorable Mention, Special Merit and finalist in numerous other contests. Her poems can be found in *The Sun*, *The Atlanta Review*, *Comstock Review*, and *New Ohio Review*, among others. Her chapbook, *Riding Waves*, can be ordered from Finishing Line Press. www.kathrynjordan.org

Jason Kahler is a teacher, writer, and researcher from Southeast Michigan. His scholarship and creative work have appeared in *Columbia Journal*, *Analog*, *Seneca Review*, *College English*, *Journal of Contemporary Criminal Justice*, *Stonecoast Review*, and other publications. www.jasonkahler.com

Brandon Kelley is a poet and library worker living in the Philadelphia area.

Becky Kennedy is a linguist and a college professor who lives with her family in Jamaica Plain, Massachusetts. Her work has appeared in a number of journals, and her poetry has been nominated for the Pushcart Prize.

Raphael Kosek's latest book of poetry, *Harmless Encounters*, won the 2021 Jesse Bryce Niles Chapbook Contest. *American Mythology*, a finalist at Brick Road Poetry Press, was released in 2019. *Rough Grace* won the 2014 Concrete Wolf Chapbook Contest. Her poems and lyric essays have been nominated for Pushcart Prizes. She served as the 2019-2020 Dutchess County, New York Poet Laureate where she teaches at Dutchess Community College. www.raphaelkosek.com

Rosa Lane is author of three poetry collections including Chouteau's Chalk, winner of the 2017 University of Georgia Press Poetry Prize, *Tiller North*, winner of the 2014 Sixteen Rivers Poetry Manuscript Competition, and *Roots and Reckonings*, a chapbook. Her work won the 2018 William Matthews Poetry Prize among other prizes and has appeared in *Asheville Poetry Review, Cutthroat, Massachusetts Review, Nimrod, Ploughshares, Rhino Poetry, Southampton Review*, and elsewhere.

Larry Leffel was on the staff of *Passages North* for many years and spent fifteen years as coordinator for the Bay de Noc Writers Conference, a week-long residency that featured such writers as Stu Dybek, Charles Baxter, William Stafford, Alice Fulton, and Eve Shelnutt. A few beers, a few burgers, lots of literary chatter, and workshops galore.

V. P. Loggins is the author of *The Wild Severance* (2021), winner of the Bright Hill Press Poetry Book Competition, *The Green Cup* (2017), winner of the *Cider Press Review* Editors' Book Prize, *The Fourth Paradise* (Main Street Rag 2010), *Heaven Changes* (Pudding House 2007), and two books on Shakespeare. His poems are in *The Baltimore Review, Poet Lore, Poetry East, Poetry Ireland Review, The Southern Review, Tampa Review*, and others. www.vploggins.com

George Looney's books include *The Acrobatic Company of the Invisible*, winner of the 2022 *Cider Press Review* Editors' Prize, *Birds of Sympathy: Correspondences* (with Douglas Smith), winner of the 2022 Apogee Poetry Chapbook Award, *The Visibility of Things Long Submerged*, which won the 2022 *BOA Editions'* Short Fiction Award, and *The Itinerate Circus: New and Selected Poems 1995-2020*. He founded the BFA Program at Penn State Erie, edits *Lake Effect*, and is translation editor of *Mid-American Review*.

Andy Macera has received awards from *Plainsongs, Mad Poets Review*, and *Philadelphia Poets*. His work has also appeared in *Pearl, California Quarterly, Drunk Monkeys, Philadelphia Stories, Straight Forward, Sierra Nevada Review, Old Red Kimono, Passager*, and other journals.

Srinivas Mandavilli is a practicing pathologist in Hartford, Connecticut, who went to medical school in India and then trained in oncologic pathology in the United States. He has had poems published in *The Raven's Perch, Indolent Books, Verse Virtual, The Night Heron Barks, Caduceus, Theodate, JAMA, Freshwater,* and elsewhere. He is also the author of a chapbook *Gods in the Foyer* (Antrim Books). He lives in West Hartford, Connecticut.

Paul Martin's poems have appeared in *America, Boulevard, Commonweal, New Letters, Poetry East,* and *Southern Poetry Review*. His first book, *Closing Distances,* was published by The Backwaters Press in 2009, and his second, *River Scar,* was published in 2019 by Grayson Books. He's the author of three prize-winning chapbooks: *Rooms of the Living* (Autumn House Press, 2013), *Floating on the Lehigh* (Grayson Books, 2015) and *Mourning Dove* (Comstock Review's Jessica Bryce Niles Prize, 2017).

Ivy McCall is a poet from Virginia. She now lives in coastal New England. She received her bachelor's degree in Global Liberal Studies from New York University, a Masters in Social Work from the University of Pittsburgh, and a C in 6th grade English. The fact that she was graded on the organization of her binder still rankles. Instagram: @ivylear Twitter: @ivy_lear

Rennie McQuilkin served as Connecticut Poet Laureate from 2015-2018. He co-founded the Sunken Garden Poetry Festival and directed it for nine years. His poetry has appeared in *The Atlantic, Poetry, The American Scholar, The Southern Review, The Yale Review, The Hudson Review,* and others. He has received fellowships from the National Endowment for the Arts and the Connecticut Commission on the Arts. He was awarded the Connecticut Center for the Book's Lifetime Achievement Award and its 2010 poetry award.

Nan Meneely's *Letter from Italy,* 1944 was noted by *The Hartford Courant* as one of thirteen important books published by Connecticut writers in 2013. It provided the libretto for an oratorio composed by Sarah Meneely and performed twice by Connecticut chorales and symphony orchestras. *Simple Absence,* published in 2020, was nominated for the National Book Award and was a grand prize finalist in the Eric Hoffer and Next Generation Indies competitions.

Erika Michael has a Ph.D. in Art History from the University of Washington. She has worked with Carolyn Forché, Thomas Lux, Linda Gregerson, Laure-Anne Bosselaar, Tim Siebles, Major Jackson, and Jeffrey Levine. Her poems have appeared in *Poetica, Cascade, Drash, Bracken, The Winter Anthology*, and elsewhere. In 2019 she won first prize for Ekphrastic Poetry at the Palm Beach Poetry Festival. Michael's first collection, *Letting Gravity Speak*, appeared in April 2023.

Larry Narron's poems have appeared in *Phoebe, Bayou, Hobart, Booth*, and *Sugar House Review*, among others. Some have been nominated for the Best of the Net and Best New Poets. Narron's first chapbook, *Wasted Afterlives*, was published in 2020 by *Main Street Rag*. A new poetry manuscript was recently recognized as a semifinalist in the 2022 Flume Press Chapbook Contest.

Sandra Salinas Newton is a Filipina-American poet and novelist and a professor emeritus of English (at Naugatuck Valley Community College) currently living in Austin, Texas. Her published work includes texts, essays, fiction, and currently poetry, in over fifty online and print journals. She was recently one of four finalists in the 2022 Writers' League of Texas Manuscript Contest (Historical Fiction category). www.snewton.net.

Eugene O'Connor's poems and translations have appeared in *arlington literary journal, The Avocet, The Awakenings Review, Classical Outlook, The Columbia Anthology of Gay Literature, Common Threads, The Comstock Review, Mead, OASIS Journal, Poetry Pacific, Pudding Magazine, Roman Poets of the Early Empire*, and elsewhere. His chapbook, *Wanderer at the World's Edge*, was named a 2021 Blue Light Poetry Prize Finalist and was published by Blue Light Press in 2022. He lives in Columbus, Ohio.

Glenn Pape is a retired man attempting to age gracefully while sharing a house in Portland, Oregon with his wife and a loveable terrier mutt who looks like a cross between Bernie Sanders and a loofah. He began submitting his writing in earnest at the age of 50 and has since been published in *North American Review, The Sun, Poet Lore, Pulp Literature, MONO*, and *The Rhysling Anthology*, among others.

Matt Pasca is a poet, educator and traveler who believes in art's ability to foster discovery, empathy, and justice. He has authored two poetry collections: *A Thousand Doors* (2011) and *Raven Wire* (2016), and has had work published in over 50 journals. Pasca served as Assistant Poetry Editor of *2 Bridges Review* and was named 2022 Long Island Poet of the Year by the Walt Whitman Birthplace Association. He has taught English to high school seniors since 1997.

Julia Morris Paul is author of *Shook*, (Grayson Books), *Table with Burning Candle*, (forthcoming in 2024 from Cornerstone Press), and a chapbook, *Staring Down the Tracks* (The Poetry Box). Her poems are widely published. "Dear Coroner, How Could You Know" appears in the 2023 *Pushcart Prize XLVII Best of the Small Presses* anthology. She serves as president of the Riverwood Poetry Series and is an elder law attorney in Manchester, Connecticut.

Pit Pinegar is the author of three books of poetry, *Nine Years between Two Poems*, *The Possibilities of Empty Space*, and *The Physics of Transmigration*. For nearly twenty years, she was a teaching artist at The Greater Hartford Academy of the Arts and The Center for Creative Youth at Wesleyan University. She directed the Sunken Garden Poetry Festival's Urban Outreach Program for eighteen years. Pinegar lives in Cromwell, Connecticut.

Among **David Radavich**'s poetry collections are two epics, *America Bound* and *America Abroad*, as well as *Middle-East Mezze* and *The Countries We Live In*. His plays have been performed across the United States and in Europe. His latest book is *Unter der Sonne / Under the Sun:German and English Poems* (2022).

Charles Rafferty has a new collection of prose poems from *BOA Editions, A Cluster of Noisy Planets*. His poems have appeared in *The New Yorker, Connecticut River Review, Ploughshares, Bennington Review*, and *The Southern Review*. He has also published the novel *Moscodelphia* and short story collection called *Somebody Who Knows Somebody*.

Gwen North Reiss is the author of a chapbook, *Notes on Metals*, and of *Paper Aperture*, an e-publication from *Pen + Brush*. Reiss writes frequently about modern architecture and art and is co-author, with Alan Goldberg, of *Oaxacan Folk Art: Response to Covid-19*, published in 2021. Her awards include the Rachel Wetzsteon Prize at the 92nd Street Y's Unterberg Poetry Center, and she has work upcoming in the 2023 *Connecticut Literary Anthology*.

Jude Rittenhouse, award-winning poet, short-story, and creative non-fiction writer, is also a teacher, speaker, and mental health professional. Her poems, essays, and articles appear widely. Awards include a Writer's Grant from the Vermont Studio Center and multiple designations as finalist for *Nimrod*'s Pablo Neruda Prize and the Tiferet Poetry Prize. Founding co-editor for the feminist literary magazine *Moon Journal* (1995-2009, archived at Smith College), Rittenhouse has spent decades helping people use their creativity to transform and grow.

George Ryan was born in Ireland and graduated from University College Dublin. He lives in New York City. Elkhound published his *Finding Americas*, as well as *Other Places, Other Times*, and most recently *Cumulonimbus*. His poems are nearly all about incidents that involve real people in real places, and they make use of straightforward language.

Abu Bakr Sadiq is a Nigerian poet. He is the winner of the 2022 IGNYTE award for Best Speculative Poetry. His work is nominated for the Rhysling Award and is published in *Boston Review, The Fiddlehead, Mizna, Palette Poetry, FIYAH, Uncanny Magazine, Augur Magazine, Fantasy Magazine*, and elsewhere. He writes from Minna. Find him on twitter @bakronline

Claire Scott is an award-winning poet who has received multiple Pushcart Prize nominations. Her work has appeared in *Atlanta Review, Bellevue Literary Review, New Ohio Review, Enizagam*, and *Healing Muse* among others. Claire is the author of *Waiting to be Called* and *Until I Couldn't*. She is the co-author of *Unfolding in Light: A Sisters' Journey in Photography and Poetry*.

Peter Serchuk's poems have appeared in a variety of journals including *Atlanta Review, New Letters, Boulevard, New Plains Review*, and other places. The author of three published collections, his most recent is *The Purpose of Things* (Regal House). www.peterserchuk.com

Alexandrina Sergio is author of three poetry collections: *My Daughter is Drummer in the Rock 'n Roll Band*, *That's How The Light Gets In*, and *Old Is Not A Four Letter Word* (Antrim House). Her poems have been widely published in journals and anthologies, and her work has been nominated for a Pushcart Prize. She served from 2015-2018 as Glastonbury, Connecticut's first Poet Laureate.

Susannah Sheffer is the author of the poetry collections *This Kind of Knowing* and *Break and Enter*, and her nonfiction books include *Fighting for Their Lives: Inside the Experience of Capital Defense Attorneys*. Her poems have appeared or are forthcoming in *Beloit Poetry Journal*, *Tar River Poetry*, *The Threepenny Review*, and other journals. She lives near the Connecticut River in Western Massachusetts.

Vivian Shipley's 13th poetry book, *Hindsight: 2020* (LaLit Press, Southeastern Louisiana University, 2022) was selected for the 2023 Paterson Poetry Prize Award for Sustained Literary Excellence from The Poetry Center at Passaic County Community College. Previous books won New England Poetry Club's Sheila Motton Award, Word Press Prize, Connecticut Center for the Book Poetry Prize, and Connecticut Press Club Award, among other awards. Shipley is the Connecticut State University Distinguished Professor Emeritus. www.vivianshipley.net

Christopher Shipman is a poet, teacher, and drummer. Recent work appears or is forthcoming in *Denver Quarterly*, *Fence*, *Iron Horse Literary Review*, *New Orleans Review*, *Pedestal*, *Poetry Magazine*, *Rattle* (online), and elsewhere. His experimental play, *Metaphysique D' Ephemera*, has been staged at four universities. *Getting Away with Everything* (Unlikely Books, 2021), in collaboration with Vincent Cellucci, is his most recent collection.

Joan Seliger Sidney is the Writer-in-Residence at the University of Connecticut's Center for Judaic Studies and Contemporary Jewish Life. Her published books are *Body of Diminishing Motion: Poems and a Memoir* (an Eric Hoffer Legacy Finalist, CavanKerry), *Bereft and Blessed* (Antrim House), and *The Way the Past Comes Back* (The Kutenai Press). *Soul House*, Sidney's translation of Mireille Gansel's *Maison d'Âme*, will be published by World Poetry Books, November 2023.

Christopher Stewart is co-author (with Quraysh Ali Lansana) of *The Walmart Republic* (Mongrel Empire Press). His poems have appeared in numerous publications and two anthologies. His work frequently addresses themes around mental illness and recovery. In 2021 he was selected as a featured poet in the Mid-America Arts Alliance's Forgotten Stories series. He was 2022 finalist for the Steve Kowit Poetry Prize. He lives in Lincoln, Nebraska.

Steve Straight's books include *Affirmation* (Grayson Books, 2022), which has won the 2023 William Meredith Award for Poetry, *The Almanac* (Curbstone / Northwestern University Press, 2012) and *The Water Carrier* (Curbstone, 2002). He was professor of English and director of the poetry program at Manchester Community College. Currently he is the poet laureate of South Windsor, Connecticut.

Maxine Susman, South Brunswick, New Jersey, has published seven poetry collections, with work appearing in journals such as the *Paterson Literary Review, Fourth River, Crab Orchard Review, Earth's Daughters, Canary,* and *The Healing Muse*. Her awards include Pushcart Prize nominations and Honorable Mentions from the Allen Ginsberg Poetry Contest. She teaches poetry at The Osher Lifelong Learning Institute of Rutgers University while writing about art, history, nature, and the more-than-human world.

Cindy Veach's book *Her Kind* (CavanKerry Press) was a finalist for the 2022 Eric Hoffer Montaigne Medal. Her book, *Gloved Against Blood* (CavanKerry Press), was a finalist for the Paterson Poetry Prize and a Massachusetts Center for the Book 'Must Read'. Her poems have appeared in *Poem-a-Day, AGNI, Michigan Quarterly Review, Poet Lore, The Journal,* and *Salamander*. She received the Philip Booth Poetry Prize and the Samuel Allen Washington Prize and co-edits *Mom Egg Review*. www.cindyveach.com

Alinda Dickinson Wasner's work has appeared in 50+ journals. She has won the Atlanta Review Prize, The MacGuffin Prize, and the Chicago Poetry Center's juried prize, among others, including Ireland's International Poetry Prize. She was nominated for the 2011 Best of the Net Award. Her collections, *Still Burning, When You Don't Know Who You Are, Kissing the Ikons,* and others, are available or forthcoming. Wasner lives and writes in metro Detroit. www.thestarvingpoet.com

Jane O. Wayne's poetry collections are *Looking Both Ways* (University of Missouri Press) which received the Devins Award for Poetry, *A Strange Heart* which received the Marianne Moore Prize and the Society of Midland Authors Award, *From the Night Album* (Pecan Grove Press), and *The Other Place You Live* (Mayapple Press). Her work has appeared in *Southern Poetry Review, Boulevard, The Baltimore Review, December, Poetry, The Cincinnati Review, Ploughshares,* and *The American Scholar.*

John Sibley Williams is the author of four award-winning poetry collections, including *The Drowning House, Scale Model of a Country at Dawn, As One Fire Consumes Another,* and *Skin Memory.* A thirty-four-time Pushcart nominee, John is the winner of numerous awards, including the Wabash Prize for Poetry, Philip Booth Award, and Laux/Millar Prize. He serves as editor of *The Inflectionist Review* and founder of the Caesura Poetry Workshop series.

Katherine E. Young is the author of *Woman Drinking Absinthe* and *Day of the Border Guards* (2014 Miller Williams Arkansas Poetry Prize finalist) and the editor of *Written in Arlington.* She translates work by Anna Starobinets (memoir), Akram Aylisli (fiction), and numerous poets from Kazakhstan, Russia, and Ukraine. Awards include the Granum Foundation Translation Prize, the Pushkin House Translation Residency, and a National Endowment for the Arts translation fellowship. She served as the inaugural Poet Laureate for Arlington, Virginia.

James K. Zimmerman is an award-winning, neurodivergent writer and frequent Pushcart Prize nominee. His work appears in *Atlanta Review, Carolina Quarterly, Chautauqua, Folio, Lumina, Nimrod, Pleiades, Rattle, Salamander,* and elsewhere. He is the author of *Little Miracles* (Passager Books) and *Family Cookout* (Comstock, winner of the Jessie Bryce Niles Prize). www.jameskzimmerman.net

Connecticut Poetry Society

Join the **Connecticut Poetry Society**, a state-wide community of poets dedicated to the promotion and enjoyment of poetry. CPS has a long tradition of excellence in publishing work of national and international, as well as Connecticut poets. Our mission is to encourage a community devoted to poetry through chapter meetings, education, and events. You do not need to be a resident of Connecticut to join.

Reap the benefits of CPS membership!

*Free copy of *Connecticut River Review*, a celebrated national poetry journal
*Quarterly CPS Newsletter of current poetry news and events
*Local Chapters for workshop and critique
*Annual Poetry Blast and open mic
*Annual Summer Picnic and open mic
*Annual contests
*Poets on Poetry educational presentations
*ConneCTions poetry readings and workshops featuring nationally-recognized poets
*Publicity for publications, readings, workshops
*Opportunity to publish poems on CPS website

Visit our website at ctpoetry.net

Join electronically via our website, or send your name, address, email address, phone, and check for dues ($30 individual, $15 student) made out to CPS to:

CPS Membership
311 Shingle Hill Road
West Haven, CT 06516.

Your membership is renewable in April – National Poetry Month!

Connecticut Poetry Society is a 501c3 organization. Member of The National Federation of State Poetry Societies (NFSPS)

Submission Guidelines for *Connecticut River Review*

Connecticut River Review, a national poetry journal, accepts submissions from February 1 through April 15.

Electronic submissions only:
https://connecticutriverreview.submittable.com/

Full guidelines can be found on the CPS website and the Submittable page.

What to send:

- Send up to three (3) original, previously unpublished poems on no more than four (4) pages in a single Word or pdf document, starting each poem on a separate page. Poems posted on social media or on personal blogs are considered previously published.

- We do not accept work that was created—entirely or partially—with AI software.

- We prefer Times New Roman font, 12 points, and left-aligned, unless formatting is part of the poem.

- Include a brief third-person bio of no more than 75 words in the cover letter section of the submission form.

- We accept simultaneous submissions. However, please notify us immediately if your work is accepted elsewhere. To withdraw part of your submission, contact us via the Messages function on Submittable. If you withdraw using the Withdraw button on Submittable, we will consider your entire submission withdrawn.

- Please submit only once during each reading period. Additional submissions during the same submission period will not be read.

Upon publication: You will receive one copy of the journal in which your work is published.

Ordering Connecticut River Review

Connecticut River Review is priced at $15.95.
Shipping and handling is $4.00.
You can get more copies by mail by sending a check made out to
CPS (or Connecticut Poetry Society) to:

CRR
9 Edmund Place
West Hartford, CT 06119

(U.S. orders only, please)
Be sure to clearly state where your order should be sent.
Connecticut River Review is also available through amazon.com.
Libraries and other institutions can order *CRR* through Ingram.

Printed in the USA
CPSIA information can be obtained
at www.ICGtesting.com
LVHW101451120923
757960LV00001B/56